HOMO SAPIENS
PART - XVII

110 FABLES FOR TODAY'S YOUNG READERS

MAWPHNIANG NAPOLEON

Dear Readers of The '110 Fables for Today's Young Readers',

We, the team behind the Homo Sapiens series, would like to extend our heartfelt gratitude to you. Your support and enthusiasm for our books have been a source of inspiration and motivation for us. Your positive feedback and encouragement have been instrumental in our journey of writing and publishing the Homo Sapiens series.

It is because of you that our books have been able to touch the lives of so many people and spread their messages far and wide. Your interest in exploring the vast area of human nature and understanding the complexities of our world has made this series a success.

We would like to take this opportunity to thank you for being a part of our journey and for your continued support. Your loyalty and love for our books mean the world to us.

We hope that our stories have been able to shed light on the truths of humanity and inspire you to be a better person for yourself and others. We are truly grateful for the chance to share our vision and messages with you.

With heartfelt gratitude,

The Homo Sapiens Series Team

Contents

Contents

Contents

Contents

Contents

Preface

In the ancient world, the fables of Aesop served as timeless reflections on human behavior and morality. Centuries later, these tales remain just as relevant, as they continue to shed light on the complexities of the human experience. With this in mind, it is with great pleasure that we present the twelfth installment in Mawphniang Napoleon's popular "110 Fables for Today's Young Readers"

Through a collection of short stories, this book invites readers to take a deep dive into the world of Homo Sapiens and examine the truths of our species in the modern era. From the importance of self-improvement to the power of kindness, these fables offer a fresh perspective on the human experience, reminding us of the universal values that bind us all together.

As we navigate a rapidly changing world, it is essential that we continue to seek understanding and knowledge of our own nature. This book provides a unique opportunity to do just that, offering a thought-provoking and insightful journey through the complexities of human behavior. Whether you are a seasoned reader of the Homo Sapiens series or are new to this talented author's work, we invite you to join us on this journey and explore the depths of human nature through the lens of these modern-day fables.

As we turn the pages of this book, we are reminded of the importance of introspection and self-reflection. Through its simple yet powerful messages, "110 Fables for Today's Young Readers" encourages us to take a step back from the hustle and bustle of daily life and consider the ways in which we interact with those around us. It challenges us to examine our actions, thoughts, and motivations, and to strive for personal growth and improvement.

At the same time, this book also reminds us of the vital role that kindness and compassion play in our lives. Whether we are dealing with friends, family, or strangers, it is our actions towards others that define us as individuals. Through its fables, this book invites us to consider the impact of our behavior on those around us, and to make a conscious effort to be kind and understanding.

In conclusion, we believe that "110 Fables for Today's Young Readers" is a must-read for anyone seeking to understand the complexities of human nature. Whether you are a student of philosophy, a lover of literature, or simply someone seeking to deepen your understanding of the world, this book offers a unique and insightful perspective that is sure to enrich your mind and soul. Get your copy today and join us as we dive into the world of Homo Sapiens and explore the timeless truths of humanity.

Sincerely,

The Homo Sapiens Series Team

Acknowledgements

First and foremost, we would like to express our deep gratitude to all the readers who have supported the Homo Sapiens series and helped make it what it is today. Your encouragement and support have been the driving force behind the creation of this latest installment, "110 Fables for Today's Young Readers"

We would also like to extend our heartfelt thanks to our publisher for giving us the opportunity to bring this book to life. Your unwavering support and belief in the power of storytelling have been instrumental in our journey.

We are deeply grateful to Aesop for his timeless fables that inspired this book. Your wisdom and insight into human nature continue to be a source of inspiration for generations to come.

Lastly, we would like to thank Mawphniang Napoleon for bringing these fables to life in a modern context and for reminding us of the importance of self-improvement and kindness. Your talent and dedication to your craft are truly inspiring.

We hope that this book will bring as much joy and inspiration to you as it has brought to us.

Sincerely,
The Homo Sapiens Series Team

Foreword

We are thrilled to present to you the twelfth installment of the popular book series, "Homo Sapiens," written by the talented Mawphniang Napoleon. This latest addition, "110 Fables for Today's Young Readers," is an extraordinary journey into the world of human nature and its complexities. The author, inspired by Aesop's fables, has crafted a collection of short stories that reflect on modern-day human experiences and deliver profound messages about self-improvement and kindness.

As you dive into the pages of this book, you will be transported to a world of fables, where each story will challenge your understanding of humanity and the human experience. Through its simple yet impactful messages, you will be reminded of the importance of being kind to others and striving for self-improvement. This book is not just a must-read for fans of the Homo Sapiens series, but for anyone who seeks to deepen their understanding of human nature.

We invite you to immerse yourself in this captivating world of fables and to join us in the journey of exploring the truths of humanity. Get your copy today, and be sure to also check out the rest of the Homo Sapiens series and other works by this talented author.

Sincerely,
The Homo Sapiens Series Team

Prologue

From time immemorial, tales have been told to educate, entertain and impart wisdom. Aesop's fables, in particular, have captivated generations with their simple yet powerful messages that still resonate today. In "110 Fables for Today's Young Readers" Mawphniang Napoleon continues this timeless tradition, taking the wisdom of Aesop's fables and updating them for the modern world.

In this collection of short stories, the author reflects on the human experience in the 21st century, exploring the complexities of human nature and reminding us of the importance of self-improvement and kindness. The fables contained within these pages will take you on a journey through modern-day experiences, and the lessons learned from each one will stay with you long after you have closed the book.

As you dive into the world of Homo Sapiens with Part XVII, be prepared to be transported to a world of fables, where you will encounter the triumphs and struggles of modern-day humanity. With its simple yet impactful messages, "110 Fables for Today's Young Readers" is a must-read for anyone seeking to understand the complexities of human nature. Don't miss this opportunity to enhance your understanding of humanity. Get your copy today and be sure to also check out the rest of the Homo Sapiens series and other works by this talented author.

The Homo Sapiens Series Team

Special Thanks For The Design Cover

My Special Thanks To You
My Love Of My Life, Clarissa Candace Giri Khyriemujat
For Your Artwork Of This Book
Of Artful 'Scout'
From The Book 'How To Kill A Mockingbird'.
My Love,
I Am The Luckiest
That I Got Your Original Artwork
Before Jean Louise Finch . Once Again Thank You My Love
Because She Would Have Admired You
For Your Creative Interpretation Of Her Iconic Story
How To Kill A Mockingbird Is Not A Literal Title
But A Metaphor For The Loss Of Innocence And The Triumph Of
Courage
Your Artwork Is Not Artful
But Art Itself
It Looks Like You Captured A Mockingbird
In Its Natural Beauty And Grace
And Gave It A New Life On The Page.
I Hope You Are Not Expecting
A Modest Compliment From Me
Or A Simple Thank You Note
You Better Prepare Yourself
For A Standing Ovation From Me
And A Kiss Under The Starry Sky.
.

.

.

Love You Loads..........

.

.

.

Mawphniang Napoleeon

CHAPTER I

The Squirrel and the Financial Planning

One day, a wise old owl approached the squirrel and said, "Squirrel, your focus on financial planning is commendable, but don't forget to also live in the moment and enjoy life." The squirrel was taken aback, he had never thought about that aspect before.

The squirrel thought about the owl's words and decided to balance his financial planning with enjoying life's simple pleasures. He continued to save and budget but also allowed himself to indulge in small treats and experiences that brought him joy.

As the years passed, the squirrel realized that the owl was right. He had found a harmonious balance between stability and security and living in the moment. He was content and happy, and his friends and family admired him for his wise ways.

The moral of the story: While financial planning is important, it is also essential to find balance and enjoy life's simple pleasures. Strive for stability and security while also taking time to live in the moment and enjoy the journey.

CHAPTER II

The Fox and Social Media

Scene: The fox is sitting on a rock, scrolling through social media on his phone. He stumbles upon the farmer's page and is envious of the attention he receives.

Fox: "Wow, this farmer is getting so much love and praise for his pictures of his produce. I wish I could be as popular as him."

The fox then has an idea and starts posting pictures of himself pretending to be a farmer. He gets a lot of likes and comments, but soon realizes that he has nothing to actually show for it.

Fox: "I thought this would be easy, but now I have all these followers expecting to see my farm. I have nothing to offer, I'm just pretending to be someone I'm not."

The fox then has a conversation with himself.

Fox: "What's the point of appearing popular on social media if I have nothing of value to offer? I need to be genuine and find my own talent, work hard and create something of value."

Original quote: "Pretending to be someone you're not can only lead to disappointment and a lack of real success."

The fox then sets off to find his own talents and passions, determined to create something of value that he can share with the world. The scene ends with the fox walking away, head held high with determination.

CHAPTER III

The Tortoise and the Hare's Social Media Race

Scene: The hare and the tortoise are sitting in front of their phones, scrolling through social media. The hare boasts about his large following and many likes.

Hare: "Look at all these likes and followers I have, I'm the most popular one here."

Tortoise: "I don't pay attention to those things, I just share what's important to me and connect with my audience."

Hare: "Well, let's see who's really the king of social media. I challenge you to a race, and this time the winner will be determined by social media engagement."

Tortoise: "I accept your challenge, I have a solid following of dedicated fans who support my content."

The race begins and the hare sprints ahead, posting pictures at every checkpoint. The tortoise steadily makes his way, posting meaningful and thoughtful content.

Original quote: "Genuine engagement is key to success on social media."

In the end, the tortoise wins with more likes, comments, and shares on his posts than the hare. The hare is shocked and realizes the importance of connecting with your audience and providing quality content.

Hare: "I never thought that quality would beat quantity, but I see now that genuine engagement is what really matters on social media."

The scene ends with the hare and tortoise walking away, both with newfound appreciation for the value of genuine engagement and quality content on social media.

The Tortoise and the Hairdresser

Tortoise: "Excuse me, hairdresser, can you give me a haircut?"

Hairdresser: "Of course! I'm the most famous hairdresser in town, you know. I'll give you the most beautiful haircut you've ever had."

Tortoise: "I've heard great things about you. I can't wait to see the results."

(After the haircut)

Tortoise: "I'm not satisfied with my haircut. It looks terrible."

Hairdresser: "I'm sorry, but I have so many customers to attend to. I had to rush to keep up with my schedule."

Tortoise: "But a good haircut takes time and effort. Rushing through it just leads to a poor result."

Hairdresser: "I understand. I'll make it up to you next time."

Tortoise: "It's not just about next time. Quality should always come first, no matter how busy you are."

The moral of the story: "Don't sacrifice quality for the sake of speed."

CHAPTER V

The Ant and the Grasshopper

Enter Caption

The conversation between the ant and the grasshopper is as follows:

Ant: "I'm sorry, I can't give you any food or money. I've been working hard all year to save for the future."

Grasshopper: "Why should I save for the future? Life is short, I want to enjoy it while I can."

Ant: "That's a short-sighted approach. You have to think about the future. What will you do when the winter comes?"

Grasshopper: "I never thought about that. I guess I need to start working hard and saving money."

Ant: "Exactly. It's never too late to start. Here, take this food and money, but remember, work hard and be prepared for the future."

Grasshopper: "Thank you, I will take your advice to heart. I promise to work hard and be prepared for the future."

CHAPTER VI

The Tortoise and the Hare in the Social Media Age

The tortoise, feeling victorious, approached the hare and said, "You were so focused on showing off your speed, you forgot to focus on the finish line."

The hare, feeling defeated, replied, "I never realized that the most important race was the one within myself. I've learned to value the journey, not just the destination."

The tortoise nodded and added, "We each have our own unique pace and style, and that's what makes us special. It's not about being the fastest, but about staying true to ourselves and working towards our goals, one step at a time."

The two friends hugged and continued on their own paths, each one grateful for the lessons they had learned from each other.

CHAPTER VII

The Boy Who Cried Wolf in the Digital Age

Villager 1: "Why did you do it, boy? Why did you cry wolf all those times?"

Boy: "I was bored, and I wanted to play a prank."

Villager 2: "But you see what your lies have led to? The wolf has taken some of our sheep because we did not believe you when you needed our help."

Boy: "I never thought it would lead to this. I'm sorry."

Villager 1: "Sorry is not enough. Words are powerful, and they can have consequences. Remember that."

Villager 2: "In this digital age, it is easy to spread false information. But we must be careful what we say and do, for the consequences can be dire."

Boy: "I will remember that from now on. I never want to be responsible for such a tragedy again."

Villager 1: "Good. The next time you have a thought or a story to share, think carefully about the impact it might have on others. For in the end, our actions define us."

Villager 2: "And as philosopher George Santayana once said, 'Those who cannot remember the past are condemned to repeat it.'"

CHAPTER VIII

The Ant and the Grasshopper in the Modern World

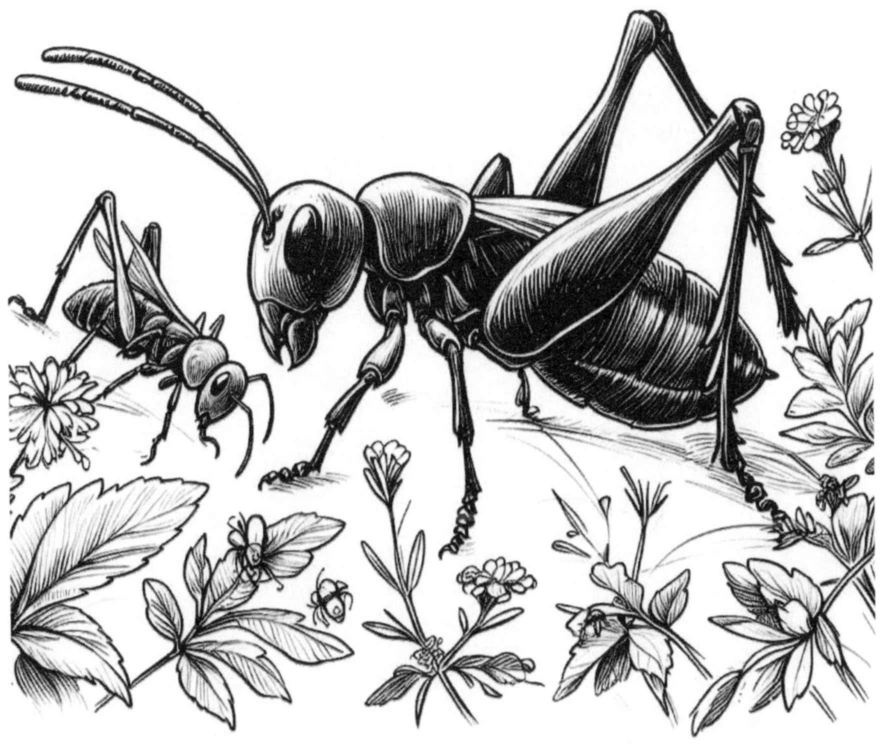

Ant: "Why did you not prepare for winter like I did, grasshopper?"
Grasshopper: "I lived for the moment, singing and playing all day. I never thought about the future."

Ant: "As the poet Robert Frost once said, 'The best way out is always through.' The future is uncertain, and we must be prepared for it."

Grasshopper: "I never thought about that. I just wanted to enjoy life while I could."

Ant: "As the author F. Scott Fitzgerald wrote, 'Too much of anything is bad, but too much good whiskey is barely enough.'"

Grasshopper: "I understand now. I should have thought about the future and prepared for it."

Ant: "Indeed. And as philosopher Aristotle once said, 'We are what we repeatedly do. Excellence, then, is not an act, but a habit.'"

Grasshopper: "Thank you for your wisdom, ant. I will make sure to live a life of balance from now on, preparing for the future while also enjoying the present."

Ant: "That is wise, grasshopper. For as poet William Butler Yeats once wrote, 'Education is not the filling of a pail, but the lighting of a fire.'"

CHAPTER IX

The Fox and the Grapes in the Online World

Act 1,

Scene 1:

(The fox is sitting under the tree, looking at the grapes hanging from the vine)

Fox: (sighs) Those grapes look so juicy and delicious, but they are just out of reach. I can't seem to find a way to get to them.

Scene 2: (The fox stands up and starts pacing back and forth)

Fox: (muttering to himself) I can't have them, but I don't want to admit that. Maybe if I tell everyone they are sour, no one will want them.

Scene 3: (The fox approaches a group of animals)

Fox: Hey guys, have you seen those grapes over there? They are sour and not worth your time.

Rabbit: (surprised) Really? I've always heard they were sweet and juicy.

Fox: (defensive) Well, I tried them and trust me, they are sour.

Scene 4: (The animals start spreading the word about the sour grapes)

Raccoon: I heard the grapes are sour, not worth trying.

Squirrel: Yeah, I heard the same thing.

Scene 5: (An old wise owl approaches the fox)

Owl: Why are you spreading false information about the grapes, my friend?

Fox: (ashamed) I couldn't reach them and I was upset. I didn't want to admit it so I said they were sour.

Owl: (wisely) Spreading false information only undermines your own credibility and discredits your character. It's better to admit when you are wrong and learn from it.

Act 2,

Scene 1:

(The fox approaches the group of animals and the vine)

Fox: I'm sorry, guys. I was wrong about the grapes. They are actually sweet and juicy. I just couldn't reach them.

Scene 2:

(The animals start trying the grapes and realize they are sweet)

Rabbit: Wow, these grapes are delicious!

Raccoon: I'm glad we didn't listen to that false information.

Scene 3:

(The fox sits under the tree, looking at the grapes)

Fox: (reflecting) I learned a valuable lesson today. It's better to admit when I'm wrong and not spread false information, even if it's to make myself feel better.

The End.

CHAPTER X

The Hawk and the Dove

Act 1,
Scene 1:
(The hawk is flying through the forest, searching for its next meal)
Hawk: (thinking to himself) I need to find something to eat soon. I've been hunting all morning and haven't had any luck.
Scene 2:

(The hawk spots the dove perched on a branch)

Hawk: (excited) Finally! I've found my next meal.

Scene 3: (The hawk swoops down to attack the dove, but the dove speaks up)

Dove: Hawk, why must you hunt me? I am a peaceful bird and do no harm to anyone. Can't we coexist peacefully in this forest?

Scene 4:

(The hawk is taken aback by the dove's words)

Hawk: (pausing) I've never thought about it like that before. I just hunt because it's what I've always done.

Scene 5: (The hawk starts to understand the value of peace and coexistence) Hawk: (softly) I suppose we can try to live together peacefully.

Act 2,

Scene 1:

(The hawk and the dove are roaming the forest together)

Dove: (smiling) It's so nice to have a friend who understands the value of peace.

Hawk: (nodding) I've learned a lot from you, dove. Hunting was a cruel and unnecessary act.

Scene 2:

(They come across a group of birds fighting)

Hawk: (stepping in) Stop! Can't we all live together peacefully?

Scene 3:

(The birds start to listen and the hawk and dove show them the value of peace and coexistence)

Owl: (impressed) I never thought about it that way before. Thank you for showing us a better way.

Scene 4:

(The hawk and dove continue to roam the forest, spreading their message of peace and coexistence)

Dove: (smiling) The forest is a better place when we all work together.

Hawk: (nodding) Indeed.

The importance of cooperation and peaceful coexistence can't be overstated.

The End.

CHAPTER XI

The Man and the Filter

Enter Caption

Act 1,
Scene 1:
(The man is sitting in front of his computer, scrolling through his social media feed)

Man: (thinking to himself) I need to find the perfect photo to post tonight. I want to show everyone how attractive I am.

Scene 2: (The man opens his photo album and starts editing his photos)

Man: (smiling) This filter will make my skin look smoother, and this one will brighten up my eyes.

Scene 3: (The man posts the edited photo on his social media page)

Man: (excited) That's it! Everyone will be so impressed.

Scene 4:

(The man arrives at the fancy party, expecting to be the center of attention)

Man: (thinking to himself) This is it. This is my chance to show everyone how amazing I am.

Scene 5:

(The man is shocked to find out that people are unimpressed with his looks)

Man: (confused) But I thought I looked so good in my photos. Why isn't anyone interested in me?

Act 2,

Scene 1:

(The man is talking to a stranger at the party)

Stranger: (politely) Excuse me, but I couldn't help but notice that your appearance is different from your social media photos.

Man: (defensive) What do you mean? I don't understand.

Scene 2:

(The stranger explains to the man that filters and editing can't replace authenticity)

Stranger: You see, people are attracted to authenticity. They want to see the real you, not just a filtered version.

Scene 3:

(The man starts to understand the value of being true to himself)

Man: (realizing) I never thought about it that way before. I've been hiding behind filters and edits, trying to impress people.

Scene 4:

(The man starts to embrace his true self)

Man: (smiling) From now on, I want to show people the real me. I want to be authentic and unique.

Scene 5:

(The man leaves the party, feeling confident and proud of who he is)

Man: (thinking to himself) Authenticity is what makes me appealing and interesting to others. I don't need filters or edits to be happy with who I am.

The End.

CHAPTER XII

The Man and the False Reviews

Scene: The man's small business is closing down. He's sitting at his desk, surrounded by empty shelves and boxes.

Man: (sighs) I thought this was going to work. I thought that by paying for those fake reviews, I could attract more customers and save my business. But now, it's all falling apart.

Friend: (enters the store) Hey, what's going on? I heard you're closing down.

Man: Yeah, it's true. No one trusts me anymore. I thought I was doing the right thing, but now, I can see how wrong I was.

Friend: Why did you do it? Why did you pay for those fake reviews?

Man: I was desperate. My business was struggling, and I thought this was the only way to attract more customers. But now, I realize that all I did was destroy my reputation and credibility.

Friend: Honesty is always the best policy, my friend. You can't build a successful business on lies and deceit.

Man: (tearfully) I know that now. I've lost everything because of my foolishness.

Friend: (puts a hand on the man's shoulder) It's not too late to make things right. You can still apologize and start over. You can build a better business, one that's based on honesty and integrity.

Man: (takes a deep breath) You're right. It's time for me to start over and do things the right way. Thank you for being here for me, my friend.

Friend: Anytime, my friend. Anytime.

CHAPTER XIII

The Fox and the Cyberbully

Scene: A forest clearing, where a large group of animals have gathered to watch a public debate between the fox and the cyberbully.

(Fox walks onto the stage)

Fox: (Speaking confidently) Good evening, fellow creatures of the forest. I am here today to address a serious issue that affects us all. Cyberbullying. (Pauses to look around the crowd) I have been a victim of cyberbullying for far too long. And I can no longer stand by and watch this harmful behavior continue.

Cyberbully: (Laughing mockingly) Oh, here we go. The little fox thinks he can take me down.

Fox: (Ignoring the bully's taunts) I have decided to confront you, (pointing to the bully) to put an end to this once and for all. I want to show everyone that we can use our intelligence and wit to stand up against bullying.

Cyberbully: (Scoffs) You're just wasting your time, fox. You can't possibly win against me.

Fox: (Smiling) We'll see about that. (Turns to address the crowd) Let's begin the debate.

(The debate begins with the fox and the bully exchanging arguments and counter-arguments. The fox uses logic and evidence to make his points, while the bully resorts to insults and personal attacks.)

Cyberbully: (Yelling) You're just a weak, scared little fox. No one cares about what you have to say.

Fox: (Steadily) That may be true for you, but it's not true for me. I have the support of my friends and family. And most importantly, I have my own self-respect. I won't let your words bring me down.

Cyberbully: (Sighs) You're making a big mistake, fox. You can't possibly win this argument.

Fox: (Smiling) On the contrary, I already have. (Turns to the crowd) By standing up to you, I have shown everyone that we can use our voices to put an end to bullying. That is the real victory.

(The crowd erupts into applause and cheers for the fox. The cyberbully looks defeated and walks away, while the fox is embraced by his friends and family.)

Moral: By using our intelligence and speaking out against cyberbullying, we can put an end to this harmful behavior. We should never be afraid to stand up for ourselves and others.

CHAPTER XIV

The Ant and the Online Scam

INT. ANT'S HOME - DAY

The ant is sitting at his desk, looking at his computer screen. He looks worried and stressed.

ANT: (sighs) I can't believe I fell for that scam. How could I have been so careless with my finances?

Suddenly, the doorbell rings. The ant gets up and goes to the door.

ANT: (opening the door) Hello?

A group of ants stand outside, looking concerned.

ANT 1: We heard what happened. Are you okay?

ANT: (shakes his head) No, I'm not okay. I lost all my savings to a scam. I should have known better.

ANT 2: Don't be too hard on yourself. Scams like these are becoming more and more common in the digital world.

ANT: (voice trembling) But I was so tempted by the promise of wealth. I let my greed get the best of me.

ANT 3: That's exactly what the scammers count on. They prey on people's weaknesses and emotions.

ANT: (sighs) I just wish I had done more research before investing.

ANT 4: That's the important lesson here. We all have to be cautious and vigilant when it comes to online transactions.

ANT: (nodding) You're right. I'll make sure to spread the word to others so they don't fall victim to scams like this.

The other ants nod in agreement, and the ant takes a deep breath, trying to calm himself down.

ANT: (smiling) Thank you for coming and checking on me. I'll be okay.

The ants smile and nod, and then turn to leave.

ANT: (calling after them) And remember, always do your research and be cautious when dealing with online transactions.

The ants nod, and the ant closes the door, feeling a little bit better knowing that he can still help others by sharing his experience.

CHAPTER XV

The Dog and the Online Addiction

INT. DOG'S LIVING ROOM - DAY
The dog, BUDDY, is sitting on the couch, eyes fixed on his phone screen.
BUDDY'S OWNER (off-screen): Buddy! Buddy, come here!
BUDDY barely reacts to the call.
BUDDY'S OWNER (off-screen): Buddy!
BUDDY finally looks up, startled.

BUDDY'S OWNER: What are you doing, Buddy? You've been on that thing for hours.

BUDDY: (defensive) I'm just, uh, checking my social media.

BUDDY'S OWNER: Buddy, you're missing out on life. You haven't even played with your ball today.

BUDDY looks down at his phone, then at the ball near his feet. He seems conflicted.

BUDDY: (sighs) I know. I just...I can't seem to put this down.

BUDDY'S OWNER: Buddy, you're addicted to the internet. You need to take a break.

BUDDY: (defensive) I'm not addicted!

BUDDY'S OWNER: Buddy, you're missing out on so much. You're neglecting your friends, your responsibilities. You're missing out on life.

BUDDY looks down, feeling ashamed.

BUDDY: (sighs) I know. I just...I feel like the internet is my escape.

BUDDY'S OWNER: Buddy, you don't need an escape from life. You need to embrace it. And that starts with putting down your phone.

BUDDY takes a deep breath and sets down his phone. He picks up the ball and looks up at his owner with a new determination in his eyes.

BUDDY: You're right. I need to start living my life, not just scrolling through it.

The dog and his owner exit the living room, leaving the phone behind.

The moral of the story is displayed on the screen: "Moderation is key when it comes to internet usage. Spending too much time online can harm our relationships and prevent us from fulfilling our responsibilities."

CHAPTER XVI

The Tortoise and the Social Media Star

Scene: A quiet park, where the tortoise is seen taking a slow walk. Suddenly, a flashy car stops in front of him, and a young and trendy social media star steps out.

Social Media Star: (laughing) Hey there! What are you doing here, little guy? You'll never be famous, you're just too slow.

Tortoise: (smiling) Slow and steady wins the race, my friend.

Social Media Star: (sarcastically) Right. Well, good luck with that. (gets back into the car)

Scene: Five years later, the tortoise is seen volunteering at a local community center, helping elderly people and playing games with kids. Meanwhile, the social media star is seen sitting alone in a dimly lit room, scrolling through their social media feeds and checking the declining number of followers.

Social Media Star: (sighs) What happened? Why did my fame fade so quickly?

Tortoise: (enters the room) Hello there! I saw you from the park and thought I'd come say hello.

Social Media Star: (surprised) Hey! What are you doing here?

Tortoise: (smiling) I've been busy, making a difference in my community, spreading joy, and helping those in need.

Social Media Star: (envious) That's great. I wish I could have done something like that.

Tortoise: (encouraging) It's never too late to start. It doesn't have to be grand, even small acts of kindness can make a big impact.

Social Media Star: (nodding) You're right. I need to focus on what's truly important.

The tortoise and the social media star continue their conversation, discussing the importance of living a slow and steady life, focusing on making a difference, and spreading joy to those around them.

The moral of the story is that fame and fortune are not the keys to happiness and success. It's better to live a slow but steady life, focusing on making a difference and spreading joy to those around us.

CHAPTER XVII

The Ant and the Smartphone

Scene: The ant is in the middle of gathering food for the winter. Suddenly, a man with a smartphone walks by and notices the ant working hard.

Man: Excuse me, little ant. Why are you working so hard?

Ant: I am preparing for the future. I want to make sure I won't go hungry during the winter.

Man: (chuckles) Why bother with all that work? Just buy food with your smartphone and have it delivered to your door.

Ant: (stops working for a moment and looks up at the man) I prefer to work hard and be self-sufficient, rather than rely on technology to do everything for me.

Man: (surprised) Really? Don't you see how much easier technology makes our lives?

Ant: Of course, I do. But there is something fulfilling about working hard and providing for yourself. It gives you a sense of pride and independence.

Man: (sighs) I suppose you're right. I've been so caught up in the convenience of technology that I've forgotten the value of hard work. Thank you for reminding me, little ant.

Ant: (smiling) No problem. That's what friends are for.

The man nods and walks away, reflecting on the ant's words. The ant goes back to work, gathering food for the winter with a sense of satisfaction.

The moral of the story is that relying solely on technology to solve our problems is not always the best solution. It's important to work hard and be self-sufficient, rather than relying on convenience and instant gratification.

CHAPTER XVIII

The Owl and the Night Owl

Act 1, Scene 1:

(The Owl is sitting in his tree, reading a book by moonlight. The Night Owl flies in, looking exhausted and disheveled.)

Night Owl: Hey there, Owl. Why are you already in bed? It's still early.

Owl: I like to get a good night's sleep so I can be alert and ready for the day ahead.

Night Owl: (laughs) Who needs sleep when you can stay up all night and have fun?

Owl: I prefer to take care of my health and be prepared for whatever life throws my way.

Night Owl: (sighs) I used to think the same way, but now I'm tired all the time and I struggle to keep up.

Act 1, Scene 2:

(Several years have passed. The Owl is sitting in his tree, looking refreshed and alert. The Night Owl flies in, looking exhausted and disheveled.)

Night Owl: (whining) I can't take it anymore. I'm tired all the time and I can't keep up with life's demands.

Owl: (concerned) Maybe you should try getting a good night's sleep like I do. It can do wonders for your health and well-being.

Night Owl: (defeated) You're right. I've been neglecting my health and now it's caught up with me. I need to make a change.

Act 1, Scene 3:

(The Night Owl has started going to bed early and waking up early, just like the Owl. He looks refreshed and alert.)

Night Owl: (grinning) I can't believe how much better I feel now that I'm getting enough sleep. Thank you for your advice, Owl.

Owl: (smiling) I'm glad I could help. Taking care of our health is important for success and happiness.

(The two friends embrace, and the stage fades to black.)

The moral of the story is that getting a good night's sleep and taking care of our health is important for success and happiness. Staying up all night and neglecting our health can lead to burnout and negative consequences.

CHAPTER XIX

The Mouse and the Hoarder

INT. MOUSEHOLE - DAY

The mouse is curled up in his bed, surrounded by a few pieces of cheese and some seeds. The hoarder enters, looking around the tiny space in disbelief.

HOARDER: (laughing) How can you live like this? You have barely anything here!

MOUSE: (smiling) I only collect what I need, and I find joy in living simply.

HOARDER: (shaking his head) You're missing out on so much. The more you have, the happier you'll be.

MOUSE: (thoughtful) I prefer to live without the clutter and stress that comes with excess possessions.

HOARDER: (skeptical) I just don't understand it. Why limit yourself?

MOUSE: (firmly) I believe that having less and focusing on what truly matters brings more joy and happiness than constantly acquiring more possessions.

The hoarder looks at the mouse, considering his words.

HOARDER: (softening) Maybe you're right. I've become consumed with collecting more and more, but I'm never truly happy.

MOUSE: (smiling) It's never too late to make a change. Let's focus on what truly matters in life and let go of materialistic desires.

The hoarder nods, a look of determination in his eyes. The two creatures sit in silence, contemplating the simple yet profound truth about what brings true happiness.

CHAPTER XX

The Mouse and the Social Media Influencer

Scene: The mousehole of the mouse and the house of the social media influencer.

(The mouse is scrolling through the social media feed of the influencer, looking envious and impressed)

Mouse: Wow, look at all those followers! The influencer has it all, a big house, fancy clothes, and a life full of adventure. I wish I could be just like them.

(The influencer walks in and notices the mouse)

Influencer: Hey, little mouse. What are you doing here?

Mouse: Oh, just admiring your life. You have it all, thousands of followers, a big house, and an amazing life.

Influencer: (sighs) If only that were true. Behind the perfect posts and the bright lights, my life is not as perfect as it seems.

Mouse: What do you mean? You seem to have everything.

Influencer: (sadly) The reality is that I am struggling with my own insecurities. I constantly feel like I have to keep up the appearance of having it all together, but the truth is that I struggle just like everyone else.

Mouse: (surprised) I never thought of that. I've been so focused on trying to copy you, that I never considered the reality behind the posts.

Influencer: That's the problem with social media. It can create false expectations and make us compare ourselves to others. But the truth is, we are all unique and we have to focus on our own journey, not someone else's.

Mouse: You're right. I don't want to spend my life comparing myself to others. I just want to live my own life and be happy.

Influencer: Exactly, and that's what's most important. So, don't be afraid to be yourself and focus on your own happiness.

(The mouse nods in agreement and leaves the influencer's house, feeling inspired and grateful)

Moral: We should be careful not to compare ourselves to others, especially on social media. Everyone has their own struggles and it's important to focus on our own life and happiness, rather than trying to copy someone else's.

CHAPTER XXI

The Turtle and the Fast Lane

Act 1: Scene 1: The turtle is minding its own business, enjoying the peace and tranquility of the slow lane. Suddenly, a group of hares comes running by, laughing and having a good time.

Hare 1: Hey turtle, why are you so slow? Why don't you come join us in the fast lane? It's where all the action is!

Turtle: I'm happy here, in my own slow lane. I like to take my time and enjoy life at my own pace.

Hare 2: But why settle for a boring life in the slow lane when you can experience the thrill of the fast lane?

Scene 2: The hares convince the turtle to join them in the fast lane, promising that they'll have a good time. The turtle, curious and wanting to experience something new, agrees.

Act 2: Scene 1: The turtle is struggling to keep up with the hares. They are exhausted and constantly running, trying to keep up with the fast pace of the fast lane.

Turtle: This is too much! I can't keep up!

Hare 3: Come on turtle, don't be so slow! We're having fun, aren't we?

Scene 2: The turtle realizes that the fast lane is not for them. They are much happier in their own slow lane, taking their time and enjoying life at their own pace.

Turtle: I've had enough. I need to go back to my own slow lane. This fast pace is not for me.

Hare 1: What do you mean? This is the life! The fast lane is where it's at!

Turtle: That may be true for you, but it's not for me. I need to live my life in a way that brings me happiness and fulfillment.

Scene 3: The turtle goes back to the slow lane and continues to live a peaceful life, taking their time and enjoying life at their own pace.

Moral: We should not try to keep up with others, especially if it's not in line with our own values and lifestyle. We should focus on finding our own pace and living life in a way that brings us happiness and fulfillment.

CHAPTER XXII

The Ant and the Online Shopper

Scene: A small clearing in the forest. The ant is sitting on a log, scrolling through an online shopping app on her phone. The online shopper enters the clearing and approaches the ant.

Online Shopper: Hi there! I see you're shopping online. I'm an expert at it. What are you looking for today?

Ant: Just trying to find something to make my life more exciting. I've been working so hard every day and I want to enjoy life a little bit more.

Online Shopper: I know exactly what you mean! Shopping online is the perfect way to do that. You can buy anything you want, anytime you want.

Ant: Really? I've never thought about that before.

Online Shopper: Trust me, it's the best way to live. You never have to leave your home and you can get everything you need with just a few clicks.

Ant: That sounds amazing! I'm definitely going to try that.

The next few weeks, the ant is seen constantly shopping online, receiving packages and admiring her new possessions.

Scene: The ant's colony, where the ants are preparing for winter. The ant is frantically searching for food.

Ant: (frantic) Where's all the food? I thought I had enough for the winter.

Colony Ant 1: You've been spending all your time and money shopping online. You haven't been gathering food like you used to.

Ant: (ashamed) I didn't realize. I thought I was just enjoying life a little bit more.

Colony Ant 2: We need to work together to make sure we have enough food for the winter. Shopping online and buying things won't help us survive.

The ant realizes the importance of balancing work and pleasure and joins the colony in gathering food for the winter.

Scene: The ant is sitting on a log, watching the colony as they work together to gather food for the winter.

Ant: (thoughtful) I learned a valuable lesson today. It's important to balance work and pleasure, and to be mindful of our resources. We should focus on the things that are truly important in life and not waste our time and money on unnecessary items.

Online Shopper: (entering the clearing) Hi there! I see you're not shopping online today. What happened?

Ant: (smiling) I realized that life is more fulfilling when I focus on what's truly important. I'm happy just being here with my colony, working together to survive.

Online Shopper: (surprised) I never thought about it that way. Maybe I should try that too.

Ant: (nodding) It's never too late to change and find what truly brings happiness and fulfillment in life.

CHAPTER XXIII

The Lion and the Social Media Influencer

Scene: The Jungle, a clearing with a rock that the lion sits on.

(The lion is sitting on his rock, staring at his phone, looking defeated)

Lion: (sighs) I just don't understand. I post the same things as that influencer and no one seems to care.

Ant: (enters the clearing) King Lion, what's wrong?

Lion: (looks up from his phone) Oh, Ant. Just this social media thing. I thought I could be a influencer like the one I saw but no one seems to care about my posts.

Ant: (nodding) I see. Do you enjoy posting those pictures and videos?

Lion: (pauses) To be honest, not really. It just seemed like the thing to do.

Ant: (smiling) Then why do it? You're the king of the jungle, everyone looks up to you. You don't need to try to fit into someone else's mold.

Lion: (thinking) You know what, you're right, Ant. I don't need to try to be like someone else. I'm proud of who I am and I should be happy with that.

(The lion stands up, stretches, and roars)

Lion: (roars) I'm the king of the jungle and I'll be happy with that!

Ant: (smiling) That's the spirit, King Lion!

(The lion walks off, back to his regal stature)

Lion: (to himself) I'll focus on what's truly important, being the best king I can be for my jungle and not waste my time trying to fit into someone else's mold.

Moral: It's better to be true to yourself and not try to fit into someone else's mold. We should be proud of who we are and not try to change ourselves for the sake of others.

CHAPTER XXIV

The Fox and the Streaming Service

INT. LIVING ROOM - DAY

The FOX is sitting on the couch, surrounded by empty pizza boxes, binge-watching his favorite show on his laptop.

FOX: (excitedly) This is the best show ever!

Suddenly, he hears a commercial for a new streaming service on the TV.

COMMERCIAL ANNOUNCER: (voiceover) Tired of limited options and constant ads on your current streaming service? Switch to StreamX and get access to all your favorite shows and movies with no interruptions!

The fox's ears perk up and he quickly turns to the TV.

FOX: (excitedly) That's it! I'm done with this service. I'm switching to StreamX!

He quickly signs up for the new service and is amazed by the selection.

FOX: (excitedly) Look at all these shows! This is amazing!

However, as he starts to watch his favorite show, he realizes that the quality is not what he expected. The picture is blurry and there are constant ads. He quickly becomes frustrated.

FOX: (frustrated) What is this?! This is not what I signed up for!

He picks up his laptop and starts to do research on the service. He reads reviews and realizes that others have had similar experiences.

FOX: (disappointed) I can't believe I wasted my time and money on this. I should have done my research first.

He turns off the laptop and puts it aside. He looks out the window and sees the sun setting.

FOX: (reflecting) I should have stuck with my old service. It may not have been perfect, but at least it worked for me.

He gets up from the couch and heads outside, taking a deep breath of fresh air.

FOX: (resolute) From now on, I'll do my research and make sure I'm not wasting my time and money on something that doesn't meet my expectations.

The fox walks off into the sunset, determined to learn from his mistake.

THE END.

CHAPTER XXV

The Dog and the Delivery Service

Scene 1

[The dog, MAX, is sitting by the door waiting for a package to arrive. He barks with excitement as he hears the doorbell ring. He runs to the door and barks happily as the delivery person hands him a package.]

MAX: [excitedly] Yes! A package!

Delivery person: [laughing] You sure love your deliveries, don't you, MAX?

MAX: [barking with excitement] I just can't help it. The excitement of receiving something new always gets me going.

Scene 2

[A few days later, MAX hears about the new delivery service and decides to try it out. He orders a new toy and eagerly awaits its arrival.]

MAX: [excitedly to himself] This new delivery service promises to deliver my package within hours. I can't wait to see how it works.

Scene 3

[A few days go by and MAX has not received his package. He becomes increasingly frustrated and begins to bark loudly.]

MAX: [angrily] Where is my package? I was promised delivery within hours!

Scene 4

[MAX receives a call from the delivery service, informing him that his package has been delayed and will take longer to arrive.]

Delivery service representative: [over the phone] I'm sorry, MAX, but your package has been delayed and won't be arriving as promised.

MAX: [disappointed] What? How can this be? I was promised delivery within hours.

Delivery service representative: [apologetically] I'm sorry for the inconvenience. We've been having some issues with our delivery system, and packages have been delayed.

Scene 5

[MAX decides to stick with the old delivery service that has always been reliable, even if it takes a little longer.]

MAX: [resignedly to himself] I guess it's better to stick with what works. I'll go back to the old delivery service. They may take a little longer, but at least I know my packages will arrive safely.

The moral of the story is clear to MAX. Quality is more important than speed, and it's better to wait for a good product than to receive a faulty one. MAX learned this lesson the hard way, but he's glad he did. He's back to his happy self, barking with excitement every time the old delivery service comes to the door.

CHAPTER XXVI

The Turtle and the Remote Worker

Scene: The turtle's home, where he is working at his desk. He looks stressed and overworked.

Turtle: (sighs heavily) This remote work program was supposed to be my ticket to even more freedom and flexibility. But it's just making my life even more stressful.

Delivery person: (knocks on the door) Delivery for the turtle!

Turtle: (groans) Not now. (opens the door)

Delivery person: Hey, how are you doing today?

Turtle: (sighs) Just trying to keep up with this new remote work program. It's not quite what I expected.

Delivery person: Really? I heard it was supposed to be the best thing since sliced bread.

Turtle: (sighs) I thought so too. But it's just one long, never-ending workday. I'm connected to my computer all the time and expected to work long hours.

Delivery person: That sounds rough. But why don't you just go back to your old way of working from home?

Turtle: (smiles) You know what? That's a great idea. I think I'll do just that.

Scene: The turtle's home, a few days later. He looks much happier and relaxed.

Turtle: (smiles) I feel like a new turtle. Going back to my old way of working from home was the best decision I ever made. I'm back in control of my time and my life.

Friend: (enters) Hey, how's the new remote work program going?

Turtle: (sighs) I went back to my old way of working from home. It's just a better fit for me. I need to choose jobs that are a good fit for my lifestyle and well-being, even if they're not the most convenient or flexible.

Friend: (nods) Wise choice. Flexibility is important, but not at the cost of your stress and well-being.

Turtle: (smiles) Exactly. It's important to remember that quality is more important than speed. And it's better to have a job that is manageable and doesn't cause undue stress and strain.

Friend: (smiles) I couldn't agree more. You're a wise turtle, my friend.

Turtle: (smiles) Thanks. I've learned that sometimes, it's better to stick with what works.

The moral of the story is that it's important to choose jobs that are a good fit for our lifestyle and well-being. Flexibility is important, but it's better to have a job that is manageable and doesn't cause undue stress and strain.

The Tortoise and the Hare in the Digital Age

Scene 1: The Challenge

(The Hare is lounging in the meadow when the Tortoise approaches him)

Tortoise: Excuse me, Hare. I've heard a lot about your speed and confidence and I was wondering if you'd be willing to race me.

Hare: (scoffs) Race you? That's a joke, right? I could run circles around you before you even make it to the finish line.

Tortoise: Maybe, but I'm willing to put my money where my mouth is. What do you say, Hare? Are you up for a challenge?

Hare: (smirks) Of course, I'm always up for a good race. Let's do this.

Scene 2: The Race

(The Hare takes an early lead, leaving the Tortoise far behind. The Hare runs with confidence and ease, but eventually, he gets tired and decides to take a nap)

Hare: (panting) I've got this in the bag. I'm so fast, I could run this race with my eyes closed. I think I'll take a quick nap before I cross the finish line.

(The Hare closes his eyes and falls asleep. The Tortoise, who has been steadily moving forward, eventually passes the Hare and crosses the finish line)

Scene 3: The Realization

(The Hare wakes up to find the Tortoise has won the race)

Hare: (stunned) What? How could this have happened? I was so confident and fast, I thought I had this race in the bag.

Tortoise: (smiling) Consistency and perseverance, my friend. You were so confident in your abilities that you underestimated the power of persistence and hard work.

Hare: (sighs) You're right. I let my overconfidence get the best of me. I thought I could take a break and still win, but I was wrong.

Tortoise: It's a lesson we can all learn from, Hare. It's important to work hard and be persistent, no matter what the challenge is. Whether it's in a race or in life, success requires consistency and effort.

Hare: (nods) I couldn't have said it better myself. Thank you for the lesson, Tortoise. I'll never forget it.

Tortoise: (smiling) Anytime, Hare. Now let's go get some rest.

(The Hare and the Tortoise walk off together, both learning a valuable lesson about the importance of consistency and hard work)

CHAPTER XXVIII

The Ant and the Grasshopper in the Social Media Era

Enter Caption

INT. ANT'S HOME - DAY

The ant is sitting in his home, surrounded by piles of food. The grasshopper knocks on the door and enters, shivering from the cold.

GRASSHOPPER: Ant, I need your help. I'm starving and I don't have any food.

ANT: I remember you singing and playing all summer long, while I was working hard to gather food for the winter.

GRASSHOPPER: I know, I'm sorry. I thought I had all the time in the world.

ANT: But now, you have to pay the consequences of your actions. You need to learn the importance of hard work and planning for the future.

GRASSHOPPER: I see that now. Can you please help me?

ANT: I'm sorry, but I have to think of my own future and the winter ahead. You need to learn from this experience and start thinking about your future, instead of just living in the present.

The grasshopper nods and exits the ant's home, dejected. He looks out into the winter landscape and reflects on his actions.

GRASSHOPPER (V.O): I was too focused on living in the moment and creating a perfect image of myself, instead of working hard and preparing for the future. I need to change my ways and start thinking about my future.

The grasshopper sets out on a journey to better himself, determined to never make the same mistakes again.

The moral of the story is that it's important to focus on the future and work hard, instead of just living for the present and creating a perfect image. Social media can make it easy to get caught up in the moment, but it's crucial to remember the importance of hard work and planning for the future.

CHAPTER XXIX

The Wolf in Sheep's Clothing in the Era of Fake News

INT. SHEPHERD'S SHACK - DAY

The shepherd, a wise and experienced man, sits by the fire, sharpening his knife. He hears a commotion coming from outside and stands up to see what's happening.

Shepherd: (to himself) What in the world could that be?

He walks outside to see a large wolf attacking one of his sheep.

Shepherd: (shouting) Stop! Leave my sheep alone!

Wolf: (disguised as a sheep) Baa, baa. I'm just a sheep like the rest of them. I wouldn't dream of hurting any of them.

Shepherd: (suspicious) You don't look like any sheep I've ever seen before. And why are your eyes so sharp and cunning?

Wolf: (laughing) Oh, that's just the way I look. I'm just a harmless sheep.

Shepherd: (determined) I don't believe you. You're a wolf in sheep's clothing.

Wolf: (smiling) Prove it.

Shepherd: (smiling back) I will. I'll watch you closely and see if you act like a sheep or a wolf.

The wolf goes about his business, pretending to be a sheep, but the shepherd is always watching, waiting for the wolf to slip up. Finally, the wolf can no longer contain himself and attacks another sheep.

Shepherd: (shouting) I knew it! You're a wolf!

Wolf: (sneering) What of it? What can you do about it?

Shepherd: (firmly) I'll stop you. I'll protect my sheep and make sure they're safe from harm.

The shepherd grabs his knife and chases after the wolf, who runs away as fast as he can. The shepherd catches up with the wolf and the two engage in a fierce battle. In the end, the shepherd emerges victorious, having protected his sheep from the wolf's deceptive ways.

Shepherd: (panting) That was a close one. I'll have to be more careful in the future.

The moral of the story is that it's important to be cautious and discerning, especially in the era of fake news. We must be diligent in verifying the sources and accuracy of information before accepting it, just like the shepherd was careful to watch the wolf and make sure he was what he seemed.

CHAPTER XXX

The Tortoise and the Hare in the Fast-Paced World

Scene: A park in the countryside, where a hare and a tortoise are standing, ready to race.

Hare: (boasting) I'm the fastest animal in the forest! There's no way you can beat me, Tortoise.

Tortoise: (smiling) I'll take that challenge.

Hare: (laughing) Alright then, let's see if you can keep up with me!

The race starts and the hare is quickly ahead. He looks back and sees that the tortoise is far behind.

Hare: (laughing) This is too easy! I'll just take a quick nap and still win the race.

The hare lays down, closes his eyes and falls asleep. The tortoise, meanwhile, steadily makes his way towards the finish line.

As the tortoise approaches the finish line, the hare wakes up, realizing that he has been asleep for too long. He quickly gets up and starts running, but it's too late. The tortoise crosses the finish line first.

Hare: (panting) How did this happen? I was so sure I would win.

Tortoise: (smiling) Consistency and perseverance will always beat overconfidence and rushing ahead.

Hare: (realizing his mistake) I was so blinded by my own pride and speed that I overlooked the importance of steady progress.

Tortoise: (nodding) It's not about being the fastest, but about being the best you can be and reaching your goals.

Hare: (sighing) I've learned a valuable lesson today. Thank you, Tortoise.

Tortoise: (smiling) Anytime, Hare. Now let's go enjoy a well-deserved rest.

The two animals walk off together, with the hare contemplating the importance of perseverance and steady progress in life.

CHAPTER XXXI

The Lion and the Mouse in the Era of Connectivity

INT. JUNGLE CLEARING - DAY

A large LION is pacing back and forth, growling in frustration. He is trapped in a hunter's net, unable to free himself. Suddenly, a small MOUSE scurries into view.

MOUSE: Lion, I've come to repay the favor you showed me when I was caught in your paws.

LION: (Surprised) Mouse! I never thought I would see you again.

MOUSE: I promised I would repay the favor, and I always keep my promises.

The mouse gnaws away at the net, freeing the lion.

LION: (Overcome with emotion) Mouse, I am forever grateful. You have shown me that even the smallest of creatures can make a big difference.

MOUSE: That's the beauty of kindness. It doesn't matter how big or small you are, the impact you can have on others is immense.

LION: (Nodding) I have learned a valuable lesson today. From now on, I will not judge someone based on their size or strength. I will treat everyone with kindness and respect, for you never know who might come to your aid when you need it the most.

The lion and the mouse walk off into the jungle, their friendship a testament to the power of kindness and the importance of helping others.

The End.

CHAPTER XXXII

The Dog and His Reflection in the World of Possession

INT. RIVERBANK - DAY

A dog stands by the edge of the river, staring at his reflection. He has a piece of meat in his mouth.

DOG: (barks at his reflection) Get away from there! That's my meat!

The dog barks and growls, but his reflection doesn't move.

DOG: (frustrated) Why won't you give it back?!

The dog opens his mouth to bark again, but the piece of meat slips from his mouth and falls into the river.

DOG: (stares in disbelief) No! That was mine!

The dog stands there for a moment, then turns and sits down with a sigh.

DOG: (whispers) Why did I have to be so greedy? I had everything I needed, but I wanted more. And now I have nothing.

The dog hangs his head and looks down at the river.

DOG: (voice trembling) What have I done?

A wise old owl flies down and lands on a nearby tree branch.

OWL: (calmly) What's the matter, my friend?

DOG: (looks up at the owl) I lost my meat. I was so greedy, I wanted more, and now I have nothing.

OWL: (nodding) Ah, I see. The dangers of greed, indeed. It's important to be content with what we have, isn't it?

DOG: (nodding) Yes, you're right. I should have been happy with what I had. I shouldn't have wanted more.

OWL: (smiling) It's never too late to learn from our mistakes, my friend. Why don't we go find you another piece of meat?

The dog nods, and the owl takes flight. The dog follows him, and the two of them head off into the distance.

DOG: (thinking) I'll never forget this lesson. I'll always be content with what I have from now on.

The dog and the owl disappear into the distance, and the camera zooms out to show the peaceful river and surrounding forest.

FADE TO BLACK.

CHAPTER XXXIII

The Fox and the Grapes in the Era of Comparison

[Scene opens with a fox sitting under a tree, looking up at a vine with grapes hanging from it. The fox is visibly upset and talking to himself.]

Fox: Those grapes are so juicy and perfect. I have to have them. [He jumps and tries to reach the grapes, but falls short] Darn it! Why can't I reach them?

[The fox sits down and starts to sulk]

Fox: They're probably sour anyway. [He stands up and walks away, trying to convince himself] I don't want them, they're not worth it.

[The scene changes to the fox walking through the forest, thinking about the grapes. He runs into a wise old owl sitting on a branch.]

Owl: Hello young fox, what troubles you so?

Fox: [sighs] It's just these grapes I saw. I wanted them so badly, but I couldn't reach them.

Owl: [nods] Ah, I see. The grapes of envy. [The fox looks up at the owl, surprised]

Fox: What do you mean?

Owl: It's human nature to want what we cannot have, and to compare ourselves to others. But it's important to remember to be content with what we have, and not to be consumed by envy and comparisons. The grapes may seem perfect, but what we already have is precious too.

Fox: [pauses, thinking] I never thought of it that way. Thank you, wise owl.

Owl: You're welcome, young fox. Remember to always appreciate what you have, and not to let envy and comparisons consume you.

[The scene ends with the fox walking away, deep in thought. The camera pans out to show the forest, and the music swells to a thoughtful and emotional ending.]

CHAPTER XXXIV

The Tortoise and the Social Media

Scene: A clearing in the forest where the race between the Tortoise and the Hare is about to begin.

(Tortoise walks onto the clearing, looking confident and determined)

Tortoise: (to himself) I may be slow, but I have a strong will and determination. I will show the Hare that slow and steady wins the race.

(Hare enters, bouncing around and boasting)

Hare: Hey there Tortoise! Are you ready to lose this race? I'm the fastest creature in the forest and there's no way you'll be able to keep up with me.

Tortoise: (smiling) I'm ready. And I have confidence in my own pace.

Hare: (laughing) Well, good luck with that! (The hare takes off at a fast pace, leaving Tortoise behind)

(Tortoise continues at his own pace, steadily making his way towards the finish line)

Tortoise: (to himself) I won't let his taunts get to me. I'll just focus on my own pace and not let anything distract me.

(As the Tortoise continues, the Hare becomes confident and takes a nap)

Hare: (muttering in his sleep) There's no way the Tortoise can catch up. I'm too fast.

(The Tortoise crosses the finish line, waking up the Hare from his nap)

Hare: (surprised) What?! How did you beat me?

Tortoise: (smiling) It's not about being fast, it's about being consistent. I just kept moving forward at my own pace, and that's what brought me to the finish line before you.

Hare: (ashamed) I never thought about that. I was so focused on being fast, I forgot to take care of myself.

Tortoise: (smiling) That's the lesson to be learned here. It's important to take things slow and steady, and not to get caught up in the race for quick success.

(The two creatures walk away, both having learned a valuable lesson)

CHAPTER XXXV

The Fox and the New Phone

Scene: The forest. The fox is sitting under a tree, looking down at his new phone. His friends, a group of animals, approach him.

Fox: Hey guys, check out my new phone! It's the latest and greatest thing on the market.

Rabbit: Wow, that's impressive. What can it do?

Fox: (struggling to figure out how to use the phone) Uh, well, I'm not sure. It's really complicated.

Squirrel: Let me see. (takes the phone and starts fidgeting with it) Oh, this is actually really easy to use. What's the problem?

Fox: (feeling embarrassed) I don't know. I guess I just got caught up in buying the latest thing without thinking about whether I could actually use it or not.

Deer: That's a common problem these days. People are so focused on having the latest and greatest things that they forget about what's actually practical.

Fox: Yeah, I just wanted to show off to everyone. But now, I feel like a fool.

Raccoon: Don't be so hard on yourself. We all make mistakes. The important thing is to learn from them.

Fox: (sighs) I guess you're right. I should have focused on what I actually needed, instead of just chasing the latest trend.

Squirrel: And that's the moral of the story. Don't get caught up in what's popular, focus on what's practical for you.

Fox: Thanks, guys. I'll remember that. (smiles and pockets his phone)

Scene ends with the animals walking away, leaving the fox sitting under the tree, looking thoughtful.

CHAPTER XXXVI

The Ant and the YouTube Influencer

Scene: A clearing in the forest. The Ant is sitting under a tree, scrolling through her social media feed. The YouTube Influencer walks into the scene and sees the Ant.

Influencer: Hey there! What are you up to?

Ant: Just scrolling through my social media feed. I've been trying to grow my following, but no one seems to be interested.

Influencer: Oh, don't worry about that. It takes time to grow your audience. But if you stick with it, the rewards can be huge.

Ant: (sighs) That's what I've been hearing, but it just doesn't seem to be working for me. I've been posting pictures of my life and my work, but no one seems to care.

Influencer: (smirks) That's because you're not posting the right things. People want to see luxury and glamour, not hard work and dedication.

Ant: (frustrated) But that's not who I am. I can't just pretend to be someone I'm not.

Influencer: (shrugs) That's the game, sweetie. If you want to make it in this world, you have to play by the rules.

Ant: (sighs) I guess you're right. I just didn't realize that this world was so shallow.

Influencer: (smirks) Welcome to the real world, where it's all about likes and followers.

Ant: (defeated) I guess I'll just stick to what I know best and keep working hard.

Influencer: (chuckles) Suit yourself. But don't say I didn't warn you.

(The Influencer walks away, leaving the Ant alone to ponder her thoughts.)

Ant: (to herself) Maybe it's time to focus on what really matters. I may not have a big following, but at least I have my self-respect and my sense of purpose.

(The Ant stands up and walks off into the forest, ready to continue her work and not let social media get in the way.)

The end.

CHAPTER XXXVII

The Wolf and the Fake News

INT. FOREST CLEARING - DAY

A group of animals are gathered, some are whispering amongst themselves, while others are staring at the wolf who just entered the clearing.

WOLF: (with a sly smile) What's going on here, my friends?

DEER: (excitedly) Have you heard the news? There's a secret treasure hidden in the forest, and whoever finds it will be the richest animal in the land!

WOLF: (raises an eyebrow) Really? Who told you that?

RACCOON: (jumps in) It was the rabbits. They heard it from the squirrels who heard it from the birds who heard it from...

WOLF: (cuts in) Hold on a minute. How do we know if this is true?

The animals look at each other, unsure of how to answer.

WOLF: (smirks) I see an opportunity here. (to the animals) How about I spread the word about this treasure, and we'll all be rich?

The animals cheer and nod in agreement.

CUT TO:

INT. FOREST CLEARING - A FEW DAYS LATER

The clearing is filled with animals, all searching for the supposed treasure. The wolf stands on a tree stump, watching with amusement.

WOLF: (to himself) This is too easy. I'll be the most powerful animal in the forest in no time.

Suddenly, a wise old owl flies down and lands on a branch next to the wolf.

OWL: (to the wolf) What are you up to, young wolf?

WOLF: (taken aback) Nothing, just spreading some news about a treasure in the forest.

OWL: (sighs) I see. And where did you hear this news?

WOLF: (nervously) From the rabbits, of course.

OWL: (eyes narrowing) The rabbits? Are you sure?

WOLF: (quickly) Yes, yes. I'm sure.

OWL: (firmly) I did some investigating and it turns out that this news is false. There is no treasure in the forest.

The animals stop searching and look up at the owl and the wolf.

OWL: (to the animals) The wolf has been spreading false information, causing chaos and confusion in our community.

The animals turn on the wolf, surrounding him and shouting in anger.

WOLF: (pleadingly) It was just a joke, I swear!

DEER: (firmly) You can't just spread false news and expect us to forgive you.

RACCOON: (nodding) We can't trust you anymore.

The wolf hangs his head in shame as the animals walk away, leaving him alone in the clearing.

WOLF: (to himself) I learned the hard way that honesty is always the best policy. Misinformation only leads to negative consequences in the end.
CUT TO BLACK.

The Tortoise and the Technology

Drama:

Scene: A dense forest with a clear path down the center. The tortoise is walking down the path, deep in thought. The hare suddenly runs up to him, huffing and puffing.

Hare: Hey tortoise, what's up?

Tortoise: Not much, just taking my time and enjoying the peace and quiet.

Hare: (laughs) That's because you're so slow, you don't have anything better to do.

Tortoise: (sighs) I'm content with my pace, it's what works for me.

Hare: (smirks) Well, I have something that will make you faster. Check this out. (Hare pulls out a brand new gadget and starts showing it off to the tortoise)

Tortoise: (looks impressed) Wow, that's amazing!

Hare: (proudly) I told you. I'm always ahead of the game when it comes to technology.

Tortoise: (thinking) Maybe if I had that gadget, I could be just as fast as the hare.

Scene: The next day, the tortoise is walking down the same path, but now he has a bunch of gadgets and technology strapped to him.

Tortoise: (struggling) This is so heavy. Why did I do this to myself?

Hare: (running up to him) Hey tortoise, how's it going?

Tortoise: (breathing heavily) Not great, I can barely move with all this technology.

Hare: (laughs) I told you, you're not cut out for this stuff.

Tortoise: (frustrated) I thought it would make me faster, but it's just slowing me down and making me more stressed.

Scene: The tortoise and the hare are sitting on a log, talking.

Hare: (sighs) I guess I've been too focused on being fast and impressing others.

Tortoise: (nodding) I feel the same way. I got caught up in trying to be like you, but it's not what I truly want.

Hare: (smiles) I think we both learned that it's not about being fast, it's about being true to ourselves and what makes us happy.

Tortoise: (smiling) Yeah, slow and steady wins the race after all.

Hare: (laughs) I guess you're right. Let's just enjoy the journey, no matter how fast or slow we go.

Tortoise: (smiling) I couldn't agree more.

The hare and the tortoise continued their conversation, both feeling overwhelmed by their own insecurities.

Hare: "I can't believe it, I thought I had it all figured out. I thought being fast and flashy was all that mattered, but it's just not enough."

Tortoise: "I know what you mean, I thought technology and gadgets would help me keep up with you, but all it did was slow me down and make me feel more stressed."

Hare: "It's like no matter how hard we try, we can never seem to get ahead. We're always chasing something, but we never seem to catch up."

Tortoise: "That's because we're always looking at things from the wrong perspective. We're always comparing ourselves to others and trying to keep up with the latest trends, but that's not what life is about."

Hare: "So what is life about, then?"

Tortoise: "Life is about finding what makes you happy, and being content with who you are. It's about finding your own pace and enjoying the journey, instead of always rushing to the finish line."

Hare: "You know, you're right. I think I've been so caught up in the race that I've forgotten to enjoy the journey."

Tortoise: "We all make mistakes, but the important thing is to learn from them and move forward. We don't have to be fast, or flashy, or have the latest gadgets. We just have to be true to ourselves and live life to the fullest."

With these words, the hare and the tortoise found a newfound sense of peace and contentment. They both learned that life is not about being fast, or flashy, or having the latest gadgets. It's about finding what makes you happy and living life to the fullest.

CHAPTER XXXIX

The Hare and the Tortoise in the Digital Age

Scene 1: The Hare and the Tortoise meet.

Hare: (laughing) Why do you walk so slowly? Don't you know that time is of the essence in this digital age?

Tortoise: (smiling) I may walk slowly, but I am taking the time to enjoy the beauty of life.

Hare: (skeptically) Enjoy the beauty of life? How can you possibly enjoy life by walking so slowly?

Tortoise: (calmly) It is not about the speed, but about the journey. I believe in taking the time to appreciate the small things and to enjoy every moment.

Scene 2: The race begins.

Hare: (excited) I challenge you to a race!

Tortoise: (accepting the challenge) I accept.

Hare quickly takes the lead but becomes distracted by his phone. The Tortoise continues to walk slowly and steadily.

Scene 3: The race ends.

Tortoise crosses the finish line before the Hare.

Hare: (stunned) How did you beat me? I am much faster than you.

Tortoise: (smiling) You may be faster, but you let your distractions slow you down. I took the time to focus on what was important, and that is why I won.

Scene 4: The Hare reflects.

Hare: (realizing the lesson) I never thought about it that way. I was so focused on getting ahead that I lost sight of what was truly important.

Tortoise: (nodding) It is easy to get caught up in distractions in the digital age. The key is to slow down, take a step back, and focus on the things that truly matter in life.

The Hare nods, realizing the wisdom in the Tortoise's words. From that day forward, the Hare decides to slow down and focus on the beauty of life, just like the Tortoise.

Scene 5: The Hare's change of pace.

Days go by and the Hare is seen walking slowly and calmly, just like the Tortoise. He has stopped checking his phone and has started to take in the sights and sounds around him.

One day, he meets a group of animals who are in a hurry, just like he used to be. They ask him why he is walking so slowly.

Hare: (smiling) I have learned the importance of taking the time to appreciate the beauty of life. It is not about the speed, but about the journey.

Scene 6: The Hare inspires others.

The other animals are amazed by the Hare's newfound wisdom and they start to follow his example. They too begin to slow down and focus on the beauty of life, instead of rushing through it.

The once fast-paced world of technology is transformed into a peaceful and tranquil place, where everyone takes the time to enjoy life's simple pleasures.

And so, the Tortoise and the Hare live happily ever after, inspiring others to slow down and focus on what truly matters in life.

The End.

CHAPTER XL

The Master and the Cat (Zen)

Once there was a zen master who lived in a monastery with his disciples. He was very wise and compassionate, and taught his students the way of zen.

One day, he found a stray cat wandering in the garden. He felt sorry for the cat, and decided to adopt it. He named the cat Mimi, and gave it food and shelter. The cat was very happy, and soon became the master's favorite companion.

The master often took the cat with him when he gave lectures or meditated. The cat would sit quietly on his lap, or curl up next to him. The master and the cat seemed to share a deep bond of understanding and love.

The disciples, however, were not so happy. They felt jealous of the cat, and thought that the master was neglecting them. They complained among themselves, saying that the cat was a distraction and a hindrance to their practice. They wondered why the master was so attached to the cat, and what zen lesson he was trying to teach them.

One day, the master announced that he was going on a pilgrimage, and would be away for a few months. He asked the disciples to take good care of the cat, and left.

The disciples saw this as an opportunity to get rid of the cat. They decided to abandon the cat in the forest, hoping that it would never return. They thought that this would please the master, and that he would praise them for their devotion.

They took the cat to the forest, and left it there. The cat was scared and confused, and tried to follow them. But they ran away, and soon the cat lost sight of them. The cat wandered in the forest, looking for food and shelter. It faced many dangers, such as wild animals, hunters, and traps. It suffered a lot, and missed the master terribly.

Meanwhile, the master returned from his pilgrimage. He was eager to see his cat, and asked the disciples where it was. The disciples lied, and said that the cat had run away. They pretended to be sad, and said that they had searched for the cat everywhere, but could not find it.

The master sensed that something was wrong. He looked at the disciples, and saw the guilt and fear in their eyes. He realized that they had done something to the cat, and that they were lying to him.

He was very angry, and scolded the disciples. He said, "You fools! You have betrayed me and the cat! You have violated the precepts of zen, and acted out of greed, hatred, and delusion! You have not learned anything from me, and you have wasted your time here!"

He continued, "The cat was not a distraction or a hindrance. It was a teacher and a friend. It taught you the lessons of compassion, gratitude, and harmony. It showed you the true nature of zen, which is beyond words and concepts. It was a living example of the zen saying, 'If you meet the Buddha on the road, kill him.' The cat was the Buddha, and you killed it!"

He then said, "I will not stay here any longer. I will leave this monastery, and find another place to teach. You are no longer my disciples, and I am no longer your master. You are free to do as you please, but you will never find peace or enlightenment. You will only reap the consequences of your actions, and suffer the karmic effects of your deeds."

He then packed his belongings, and left the monastery. He never returned, and never saw the cat again.

The disciples were shocked and ashamed. They realized their mistake, and regretted their actions. They tried to find the cat, and apologize to the master. But it was too late. The cat was gone, and the master was gone. They had lost both.

They remained in the monastery, but they were unhappy and restless. They could not forget the cat, and the master. They could not practice zen, and they could not attain enlightenment. They lived in misery and remorse, until the end of their days.

CHAPTER XLI

The Social Media Bee and the Flower Garden

Scene 1: Buzz stumbles upon the beautiful garden.

Buzz is flying through a field of flowers when he sees something that catches his eye. It's a garden filled with the most beautiful flowers he has ever seen. He lands on a flower and admires its beauty.

Buzz: (whispering to himself) This is too good to be shared. I have to keep this a secret and show it off to everyone on social media.

Scene 2: Buzz shares the garden on social media.

Buzz posts pictures of the garden on his social media and brags about how he found it all by himself. His friends are amazed and jealous of the beauty that he has discovered.

Scene 3: The rumors start to spread.

Buzz's friends start to spread rumors about him, saying that he is selfish and doesn't share the beauty of the garden. Buzz starts to notice that his friends are avoiding him and he realizes that he has lost their friendship.

Scene 4: Buzz's realization.

Buzz is sitting in his garden, feeling alone and sorry for himself. He realizes that his love for social media and his desire to be popular has led him to forget the importance of true friendship and the beauty of sharing.

Buzz: (tearfully) I never meant to hurt anyone. I just wanted to be popular and show off my discovery. But now I see that my love for social media has blinded me to the true beauty of life, which is sharing and friendship.

Scene 5: Buzz shares the garden with his friends.

Buzz decides to share the garden with his friends and invite them to come and see it with him. His friends are surprised and overjoyed that Buzz is willing to share such a beautiful place with them.

Scene 6: The beauty of sharing.

As they fly through the garden, Buzz's friends are amazed by the beauty of the flowers. They share the experience together, admiring the colors, the fragrance, and the happiness that the garden brings.

Buzz: (smiling) I realize now that the true beauty of life is not in keeping it all to myself, but in sharing it with others.

Scene 7: The restored friendship.

The friends forgive Buzz and their friendship is restored. They promise to always share the beauty of life with each other, no matter what.

The End.

The Selfie Stick and the Mountain View

Snap stood at the base of the mountain, looking up at the breathtaking view. He could see the sun slowly rising over the peaks and casting a golden glow over the landscape. He quickly reached for his camera and started snapping away.

As Snap was taking his selfies, he suddenly heard a voice behind him. "Why are you so focused on taking pictures?" the voice asked.

Snap turned around to see an old man, who looked like a wise sage, standing there. "I'm taking selfies so I can share this beautiful view with my friends on social media," Snap replied.

"But are you really experiencing the view?" the old man asked. "Or are you just capturing it for others to see?"

Snap was taken aback by the old man's words. He had never thought about it that way before. He realized that he was so focused on taking the perfect picture that he wasn't even enjoying the moment.

"I want to share this experience with others," Snap said, "but I don't want to miss out on the beauty of it all."

The old man smiled and nodded. "It's all about finding a balance," he said. "You can take pictures and share your experiences with others, but don't forget to live in the moment and enjoy what you see."

Snap took the old man's words to heart and put his camera away. He spent the rest of the day taking in the beauty of the mountain and experiencing the moment. When he got home, he shared his experiences and pictures with his friends, but he never forgot the lesson he learned that day. He realized that it was more important to appreciate and experience life, rather than just capturing it for social media.

CHAPTER XLIII

The Tortoise and the Hare's Social Media Race

Scene: The Tortoise and the Hare are at the starting line of the race, surrounded by a small crowd of animals who are there to witness the event.

Hare: (excitedly) This is it, the moment I've been waiting for! I'm going to win this race and show everyone just how popular I am! (strikes a pose and snaps a selfie)

Tortoise: (calmly) I don't need to show off to win. I just want to run my race and do my best.

Hare: (laughing) Oh, Tortoise, you're so cute with your simple dreams. You'll never be able to keep up with me and my followers!

The race starts and the Hare quickly takes the lead, but stops several times to take selfies and post updates on social media. The Tortoise continues at a steady pace, focusing on the race.

Tortoise: (thinking to himself) I don't need to show off or prove anything to anyone. I just want to do my best and enjoy the journey.

As the Hare reaches the halfway point, he starts to tire. He realizes that he has wasted too much time on social media and doesn't have enough energy to finish the race.

Hare: (panting) Wait, I can't do this... I'm too tired... (looks at his phone) I should have focused more on the race and less on my followers...

The Tortoise crosses the finish line first, winning the race to the cheers of the crowd. The Hare arrives soon after, exhausted and defeated.

Tortoise: (smiling) Well done, Hare. You gave it your all.

Hare: (ashamed) I'm sorry, Tortoise. I let my desire for popularity on social media distract me from what was truly important.

Tortoise: (kindly) Don't be sorry. We all make mistakes. The important thing is to learn from them and move forward.

The animals gather around the Tortoise and Hare, congratulating the Tortoise on his win. The Hare realizes that true success and happiness come from focusing on what truly matters, rather than seeking popularity on social media.

CHAPTER XLIV

The Crow and the Smartphone

Scene 1:
(The Crow and the Bird are in the forest)
Crow: Hello there, what is that you're holding in your hand?
Bird: This? It's my smartphone. I use it to stay connected to my friends on social media and check my emails.
Crow: Can I try it? I've never seen anything like it before.

Bird: Sure, here you go.

Scene 2:

(The Crow is now addicted to her smartphone, neglecting her duties as a mother and a bird)

Crow: (Checking her smartphone) Oh, I have a new message from a friend. (Keeps scrolling)

Young Crow: Mama, Mama, where have you been? I'm hungry.

Crow: (Looks up from her phone) Oh, I'm sorry sweetie. I've been so busy on my smartphone that I forgot to gather food for you.

Scene 3:

(The Crow realizes the negative impact of her smartphone addiction)

Crow: (Thinking) What have I done? I've neglected my duties as a mother and a bird. I'm always stressed and overwhelmed.

Bird: Are you okay, Crow? You seem worried.

Crow: I've realized that my addiction to my smartphone has led to a disconnection from real life and real relationships. I need to find a balance between technology and real-life connections.

Bird: You're right, Crow. It's important to find that balance.

Crow: (Resolves) From now on, I will make sure to put my duties and relationships first and use my smartphone in moderation.

The End.

CHAPTER XLV

The Elephant and the Gratitude

INT. A JUNGLE - DAY

The elephant, named Ellie, is walking through the jungle, taking in all of its beauty. Suddenly, she stops and turns to address the audience.

ELLIE: You know, life can be so beautiful when you take the time to appreciate it. I used to take everything for granted, but I learned that gratitude is the key to happiness and contentment.

She begins to walk again, but stops once more.

ELLIE: I used to be just like that bird over there, constantly looking for the next best thing, never satisfied with what I had. But one day, I realized that I was missing out on so much of life's beauty by not taking the time to appreciate what was right in front of me.

She gestures to a bird flying overhead, checking its smartphone. Ellie pauses for a moment, looking up at the bird before continuing.

ELLIE: That's when I made a conscious effort to express gratitude for the things in my life. I started by acknowledging the small things - the sun shining on my skin, the taste of fresh water, the laughter of my friends.

Ellie smiles as she remembers these things.

ELLIE: And you know what? It made all the difference. I found that I was happier and more content with my life. I stopped taking things for granted and was able to truly appreciate all of the beauty that surrounded me.

Ellie turns to the audience once more.

ELLIE: So, my friends, the moral of the story is this: gratitude is important for happiness and contentment. Make a conscious effort to acknowledge and express gratitude for the things you have in your life, and never take anything for granted.

Ellie nods her head, satisfied with her message, before continuing on her walk through the jungle.

CHAPTER XLVI

The Squirrel and the Financial Planning

Scene: A forest, where a group of animals have gathered to hear the wise words of the squirrel. The animals include rabbits, deer, and birds, who are all eager to learn about the squirrel's financial planning skills.

Squirrel: (standing on a rock, addressing the crowd) Good morning, my friends. Today, I want to talk about the importance of financial planning. You see, I once lived in a world where financial planning was crucial.

Deer: (nodding in agreement) Yes, I have heard that you are quite knowledgeable about financial planning.

Squirrel: (smiling) Yes, I learned the hard way that if you don't plan for the future, you will be burdened by debt and financial stress. So, I made a conscious effort to live within my means, save and invest for the future, and avoid debt and financial stress.

Rabbit: (raising his hand) How did you do that, Squirrel? I have been struggling with financial planning for years.

Squirrel: (nodding understandingly) I understand, Rabbit. It's not easy, but it's important to have a plan. You need to track your expenses, set financial goals, and make a budget. And most importantly, you need to live within your means and avoid taking on debt.

Bird: (chirping) But what if you have an emergency, like a medical expense or a natural disaster?

Squirrel: (smiling) That's why it's important to have an emergency fund. You should always have a few months' worth of living expenses saved in case of an emergency. That way, you won't have to rely on debt or loans.

Deer: (impressed) That's amazing, Squirrel. I will definitely start following your advice.

Squirrel: (smiling) Good! Financial planning takes time and discipline, but the reward is worth it. You will be able to live a secure and financially stable life, without worrying about money.

Moral: (as the scene ends) Financial planning is important for security and stability. Make a conscious effort to live within your means, save and invest for the future, and avoid debt and financial stress.

CHAPTER XLVII

The Fox and the Adaptability

INT. A FOX DEN - DAY

The fox is sitting by the entrance to his den, looking out at the forest around him. He is deep in thought.

FOX: (To himself) I've learned so much since I've been in this world. I've learned the importance of adaptability. It's what separates those who thrive from those who struggle.

Suddenly, there's a rustling in the bushes and a rabbit pops out.

RABBIT: Hey there, fox. What are you so deep in thought about?

FOX: Just thinking about the importance of adaptability. It's been a game-changer for me.

RABBIT: Really? Can you tell me more about it?

FOX: Sure, I used to be like most other animals around here. Rigid, resistant to change. But then I realized that things are always changing. The weather, the seasons, the prey. If I wanted to survive, I needed to change with them.

RABBIT: I see your point. But how did you actually make the change?

FOX: It wasn't easy. It took a lot of effort and a lot of mistakes. But I made a conscious effort to be flexible and open-minded. I tried new things, I approached situations with a different perspective. And over time, I got better at adapting to change.

RABBIT: And what was the result of all this?

FOX: I'm living a successful and fulfilling life now. I'm not burdened by rigidity and resistance to change. I'm able to thrive, no matter what life throws my way.

RABBIT: That's incredible. I could use some of that adaptability myself.

FOX: It's not easy, but it's worth it. Make a conscious effort to be flexible and open-minded. Embrace change, don't resist it. That's the key to success and fulfillment.

RABBIT: Thanks for the advice, fox. I'll definitely keep that in mind.

The rabbit hops off, leaving the fox to his thoughts once again.

FOX: (To himself) Adaptability. It's what separates the winners from the losers. I'll never forget that.

The fox looks out at the forest, ready for whatever changes come his way.

Scene: The fox is sitting in his den, reflecting on his life and experiences. A young cub walks in, eager to learn from the wise fox.

Young Cub: Excuse me, sir. I've heard that you're a very adaptable fox. Can you teach me how to be like you?

Fox: Of course, young one. I'd be happy to share my experiences with you.

Young Cub: Thank you! I really want to be successful and fulfilled like you.

Fox: Well, the first thing you need to understand is that adaptability is key. The world is constantly changing, and if you can't change with it, you'll get left behind.

Young Cub: But how do I become adaptable?

Fox: You have to be flexible and open-minded. You have to be willing to try new things and embrace change, even if it's scary or uncomfortable.

Young Cub: That sounds scary. What if I fail?

Fox: Failure is a part of the learning process. If you're not failing, it means you're not taking risks and trying new things. And without taking risks, you'll never reach your full potential.

Young Cub: I see. But what if I don't know what to do?

Fox: That's when you have to be resourceful and creative. You have to be able to find new solutions and come up with new ideas. You can't be rigid and stuck in your ways.

Young Cub: I understand. Thank you for your advice, sir.

Fox: You're welcome, young one. Just remember, adaptability is a journey, not a destination. Keep learning and growing, and never be afraid to try new things.

The young cub nods and leaves the den, eager to put the fox's advice into practice. The fox smiles, knowing that the young cub is on his way to a successful and fulfilling life, full of adaptability and growth.

CHAPTER XLVIII

The Giraffe and the Confidence

Scene: A group of animals are gathered in the savanna, discussing their life experiences and the challenges they face. The giraffe walks into the conversation.

Giraffe: Hello everyone! What are we talking about today?

Elephant: We're talking about confidence and the importance of self-assurance.

Giraffe: Ah, that's a topic close to my heart. I used to struggle with confidence and self-doubt, but I learned the importance of believing in myself and my abilities.

Hippopotamus: How did you make that shift?

Giraffe: Well, I realized that confidence is not something that comes naturally to everyone. It's something that we have to work on and develop over time. I started by setting small goals for myself and celebrating my successes, no matter how small they were. This helped me build my confidence and self-esteem.

Lion: That's great, but what about when things don't go as planned? How do you stay confident then?

Giraffe: It's not always easy, but I remind myself of my past successes and that I have the ability to overcome any obstacle. I also surround myself with positive and supportive individuals who uplift me and help me maintain a confident outlook.

Zebra: That's really insightful, giraffe. Your approach to confidence has clearly paid off, you're one of the most successful animals in the savanna.

Giraffe: Yes, having confidence has allowed me to live a fulfilling and successful life. But most importantly, it's allowed me to be happy and enjoy the journey, without being held back by self-doubt or insecurity.

Moral: Confidence is key for success and fulfillment. Believe in yourself and your abilities, surround yourself with positivity and never give up on your journey.

CHAPTER XLIX

The Monkey and the Creativity

Act 1:

Scene 1: The monkey is sitting on a tree branch, looking out into the vast expanse of the forest. Suddenly, he sees a group of animals playing a game he has never seen before. They are all laughing and having a great time.

Monkey: (Thinking to himself) I've been living in this forest for as long as I can remember, but I've never seen this game before. It's new and different.

Scene 2: The monkey decides to approach the group of animals and ask them about the game. They welcome him with open arms and explain the rules. The monkey is fascinated and joins in the game. He quickly realizes that the game requires a lot of creativity and imagination.

Monkey: (Excited) This is amazing! I've never played anything like this before. It's so much fun!

Scene 3: After the game, the monkey can't stop thinking about how much fun he had. He realizes that he has been living a mundane and conventional life. He decides to make a change.

Monkey: (Determined) I need to start being more creative and innovative in my approach to life. I can't keep living a boring and conventional life.

Act 2:

Scene 1: The monkey starts to make small changes in his daily routine. He begins to experiment with new things and approaches to life. He finds that being creative and innovative brings him joy and fulfillment.

Monkey: (Happily) I've never felt so alive! Being creative and innovative is so much fun!

Scene 2: The monkey meets a group of animals who are rigid and resistant to change. They are skeptical of his new approach to life.

Animal 1: (Skeptically) What do you mean you're being more creative and innovative? That's not the way things are done.

Animal 2: (Rigidly) We've always done things this way. Why change now?

Scene 3: The monkey tries to explain the benefits of being creative and innovative, but the other animals are not convinced.

Monkey: (Persuasively) Don't you see? Being creative and innovative brings joy and fulfillment. It's not about changing the way things are done, it's about finding new and better ways to do things.

Animal 1: (Unconvinced) I don't know, it just seems like a lot of extra work.

Scene 4: The monkey decides to show the other animals the benefits of being creative and innovative. He sets up a series of challenges and games that require imagination and creativity. The other animals reluctantly participate, but they quickly realize how much fun they are having.

Animal 2: (Surprised) I never thought I'd enjoy this, but it's so much fun!

Scene 5: The other animals start to see the value of being creative and innovative, and they begin to embrace the monkey's approach to life.

Animal 1: (Sincerely) I'm sorry I was skeptical. You're right, being creative and innovative brings joy and fulfillment.

Animal 2: (Gratefully) Thank you for showing us the way. We'll never go back to our old ways.

Act 3:

Scene 1: The monkey continues to live a fulfilling and exciting life, embracing creativity and innovation at every turn. He is happy and content.

The monkey was happy with his life and enjoyed exploring his imagination every day. He would often spend hours lost in his thoughts, coming up with new and exciting ideas. His friends and family noticed how much he had changed and how much he had grown as a person.

One day, the monkey was approached by a group of animals who were looking for a creative solution to a problem they were facing. They were in a drought and their crops were failing, and they needed to find a way to save their food supply. The monkey was eager to help and suggested using rain barrels to collect and store rainwater.

The animals were skeptical at first, but the monkey was determined to help and showed them how to create the rain barrels. The animals were amazed at how effective the solution was and thanked the monkey for his help. The monkey was filled with pride and happiness, knowing that his creativity had helped solve a problem and make a positive impact on the lives of others.

The moral of the story is that creativity can be used to solve problems and make a positive impact on the lives of others. By being imaginative and innovative, we can find solutions to challenges and make the world a better place.

CHAPTER L

The Owl and the Education

INT. THE FOREST - DAY

An Owl named WISE sits on a tree branch, reading a book. Suddenly, a group of birds fly by.

BIRD 1: Hey Wise, what are you doing?

WISE: I'm reading a book, expanding my knowledge and educating myself.

BIRD 2: (sarcastically) Oh wow, how exciting.

WISE: (ignoring the sarcasm) It is exciting. Education is important for fulfillment and success.

BIRD 3: (confused) Really? I don't see how it's relevant to us birds. We just fly around and sing all day.

WISE: (serious) That may be true, but education is not just about academics. It's about learning new things, gaining new skills, and expanding your mind.

BIRD 1: (impressed) Hmm, I never thought about it that way.

WISE: (passionate) I have made a conscious effort to continuously educate myself, and it has helped me live a fulfilling and successful life.

BIRD 2: (sincere) Wise, I have to admit, you're wise for a reason. I want to be like you and never stop educating myself.

WISE: (smiling) That's the spirit! Remember, education is a lifelong journey. You never stop learning.

BIRD 3: (determined) You're right. I want to live a fulfilling and successful life too. I'll make a conscious effort to educate myself.

WISE: (proud) That's great to hear. Remember, ignorance is limiting. But with education, you can achieve anything you set your mind to.

The birds fly off, inspired and determined to continuously educate themselves. Wise watches them go, a smile on his face.

WISE (V.O): The moral of the story is that education is important for fulfillment and success. Make a conscious effort to acquire knowledge and gain new skills, and never stop educating yourself.

[Scene: The owl sits on a branch, deep in thought. A bird approaches and greets him.]

Bird: Hey Owl, what's on your mind today?

Owl: [sighs] I was just thinking about the importance of education.

Bird: Education? What do you mean?

Owl: [looks up] I've come to realize that education is key to fulfilling and successful life. Without it, we're limited by ignorance and can never reach our full potential.

Bird: [surprised] Really? I never thought of it that way.

Owl: [nods] Absolutely. That's why I make a conscious effort to continuously educate myself. I read, I listen, I learn. And I never stop.

Bird: [thoughtful] That makes sense. But what about those who don't have access to education or resources to acquire knowledge?

Owl: [serious] That's a great point, and it's a tragedy that not everyone has access to education. But even with limited resources, it's possible to educate oneself. The world is full of knowledge, and all it takes is a curious and determined mind to seek it out.

Bird: [nodding] You're right. I never thought about it that way. I'll have to start making a conscious effort to educate myself too.

Owl: [smiling] That's the spirit! Remember, education is a lifelong journey, and it's never too late to start.

[The scene ends with the bird flying off, inspired by the owl's words, while the owl continues to gaze out into the distance, deep in thought.]

CHAPTER LI

The Rabbit and the Patience

Scene: A clearing in the forest. The rabbit is sitting in front of his burrow, looking worried. The owl flies down and lands beside him.

Owl: Hello, my friend. What's bothering you?

Rabbit: I just don't know how to be patient. Everything in this world seems to be moving so fast, and I find myself getting caught up in the rush.

Owl: Ah, I understand. It can be difficult to slow down and be patient when everything around us seems to be moving so quickly.

Rabbit: Yes, I feel like I'm always rushing and never taking the time to enjoy the little things in life. And I know that impatience is causing me stress and anxiety.

Owl: Patience is indeed a valuable quality. It helps us avoid getting caught up in the rush, and allows us to take the time to appreciate the world around us.

Rabbit: But how do I learn to be patient?

Owl: It takes practice, my friend. You must make a conscious effort to slow down and take things one step at a time. It can be helpful to take deep breaths, and to remind yourself that everything will work out in its own time.

Rabbit: That's easier said than done.

Owl: I know, but I believe in you. You have the strength and determination to develop this important quality. And once you have mastered patience, you will find that you are able to live a stress-free and peaceful life.

Rabbit: You're right. I will try to be patient and take things one step at a time. Thank you for your advice, my friend.

Owl: Anytime, my friend. And remember, the journey to becoming patient is one of self-discovery and growth. Embrace it, and you will find that the rewards are well worth it.

Rabbit: I will. Thank you.

Scene ends with the rabbit closing his eyes, taking a deep breath, and focusing on being patient. The owl flies off into the sky, leaving the rabbit alone with his thoughts. The moral of the story is clear: patience is important for peace and calm. Make a conscious effort to be patient, and avoid being rushed or impulsive in all aspects of your life.

CHAPTER LII

The Tortoise and the Perseverance

INT. A forest clearing - DAY

The tortoise is taking a slow and steady walk, when he comes across a group of animals gathered around a tree. They are discussing the different ways they approach challenges in their lives. The tortoise approaches the group and listens in.

Rabbit: "I just try to stay calm and not get too worked up. Patience is key."

Fox: "For me, it's all about being flexible and open-minded. That way, I can adapt to any situation that comes my way."

Monkey: "I think it's all about being creative. You need to think outside the box and come up with unique solutions to problems."

The animals turn to the tortoise, who has been quietly listening.

Owl: "Tortoise, what is your approach to challenges?"

Tortoise: "Perseverance. I never give up, no matter how difficult a situation may seem. I keep pushing forward, step by step."

The animals nod in agreement, impressed by the tortoise's determination.

Squirrel: "But how do you keep going, even when it seems like there's no end in sight?"

Tortoise: "It's all about having a goal in mind and never losing sight of it. I know that if I keep pushing forward, I will eventually reach my destination. And even if I don't, the journey itself is still worth it."

Elephant: "That's true. And it's also about being grateful for what you have and what you've accomplished, no matter how small it may seem."

The animals all nod in agreement, realizing the value of perseverance and gratitude in their own lives.

Tortoise: "Never give up, keep pushing forward, and always be grateful. That's the key to a fulfilling and successful life."

The animals all nod in agreement, and the tortoise continues on his slow and steady journey, never losing sight of his goal and never giving up in the face of adversity.

Moral: Perseverance is important for success and fulfillment. Make a conscious effort to persist and keep going no matter what challenges you face, and avoid giving up in the face of adversity.

CHAPTER LIII

The Wolf and the Responsibility

Scene: The wolf is sitting by a fire in the woods, deep in thought. A younger wolf approaches him, looking concerned.

Young Wolf: Hey, are you okay? You seem worried.

Wolf: I am. I've been thinking a lot lately about responsibility and what it means to be responsible.

Young Wolf: Responsibility? What's that?

Wolf: It's about being accountable for your actions and taking care of your duties and obligations. It's about being trustworthy and respected.

Young Wolf: I don't understand. Why does that matter?

Wolf: Because without responsibility, we can't build trust with others. And without trust, we can't have meaningful relationships or live a fulfilling life.

Young Wolf: But what if we make mistakes? What if we can't always be responsible?

Wolf: That's part of being responsible too. Owning up to our mistakes and making amends for them. It takes courage and humility to admit our flaws and take responsibility for our actions.

Young Wolf: I see. I want to be responsible like you. Can you help me?

Wolf: Of course. It's a journey, not a destination. And the more we practice being responsible, the easier it becomes. Start small, by keeping your promises and following through on your commitments. And don't be afraid to ask for help when you need it.

Young Wolf: Thanks, I will. You're a great mentor, Wolf.

Wolf: You're welcome. Remember, responsibility is essential for respect and trustworthiness. And those are the foundation of a fulfilling life.

(The fire crackles, and the two wolves sit in silence, reflecting on the importance of responsibility.)

CHAPTER LIV

The Lion and the Leadership

Scene: The lion is in a deep conversation with a group of animals in the jungle, discussing the importance of leadership.

Lion: (with conviction) My friends, I once lived in a world where leadership was only valued in words. But I learned that true leadership is not just about having followers, it's about having a purpose and a vision. It's about making the difficult decisions and being accountable for the outcomes.

Giraffe: (nodding) I agree, lion. But it's not always easy to lead with integrity and vision, especially when the path ahead is unclear.

Lion: (firmly) That's true, Giraffe. But that's where perseverance comes in. A leader must be willing to stick to their beliefs and values, even when it's challenging. And they must have the determination to keep pushing forward, even when the road ahead is uncertain.

Deer: (thoughtfully) And what about being a strong and effective leader? How do you do that?

Lion: (smiling) That's where the true test of leadership lies. A strong and effective leader is one who can bring people together and inspire them to achieve a common goal. They must have the ability to communicate their vision and guide their followers towards success.

Hippo: (skeptically) But what if the followers don't agree with the leader's vision?

Lion: (thoughtfully) That's where adaptability comes in. A good leader must be open-minded and flexible, and be willing to adjust their approach if needed. They must be able to listen to their followers and make changes that will benefit everyone.

Raccoon: (excitedly) That's so inspiring, lion! I never thought about leadership in that way before.

Lion: (smiling) That's the beauty of education, my friend. It allows us to see things in a new light and gain a deeper understanding of the world around us.

All Animals: (in unison) Thank you, lion. We will strive to be responsible and patient, to persevere and be adaptable, and to lead with integrity and vision.

Lion: (proudly) Remember, my friends, never take anything for granted. Be grateful for the opportunity to learn and grow, and always strive to be the best versions of yourselves.

Moral: Leadership is about having a purpose and vision, persevering through challenges, being open-minded and adaptable, and being accountable and responsible. Make a conscious effort to lead with integrity and vision, and never take your opportunities for growth and development for granted.

The Fox and the Adaptability

Scene: A forest clearing, where a group of animals have gathered to discuss their experiences. The fox is sitting in the center, surrounded by the other animals.

Fox: Friends, I want to share a story about adaptability. You see, I once lived in a world where change was constant, and those who were able to adapt to new circumstances were the ones who thrived.

Rabbit: That's interesting, Fox. Can you tell us more about your experiences?

Fox: Of course, Rabbit. You see, I realized early on that being rigid and resistant to change would only lead to failure. I made a conscious effort to be flexible and open-minded, and to embrace change whenever it came my way.

Lion: That's a wise attitude, Fox. But what challenges did you face along the way?

Fox: Oh, there were many challenges, Lion. The world is constantly evolving, and those who can't keep up are left behind. But I never let that deter me. I remained adaptable, and always found new and innovative solutions to the problems I faced.

Tortoise: That's impressive, Fox. Perseverance and determination are important qualities, but adaptability is what sets you apart.

Owl: Indeed, Tortoise. Education and knowledge are important, but being able to apply that knowledge in new and creative ways is what truly sets one apart.

Squirrel: And don't forget the importance of financial planning, Owl. Being adaptable doesn't mean living recklessly or without purpose. It's about finding balance and being able to adjust your plans as needed.

Wolf: That's right, Squirrel. Responsibility and leadership are also important qualities to cultivate. Being an effective leader means being able to adapt to new circumstances, and make decisions that are in the best interest of those you lead.

Rabbit: So, what can we all learn from Fox's experiences?

All animals: Adaptability is important for thriving and growth. Make a conscious effort to be flexible and able to change with the times, and avoid being stuck in old ways of thinking.

Fox: Exactly. Embrace change, be open-minded, and always look for new and innovative solutions to the challenges you face. That's the key to living a fulfilling and dynamic life.

Scene: The fox is sitting in front of a tree, deep in thought. Suddenly, a young rabbit hops up to him.

Rabbit: Hello, Mr. Fox. What are you thinking about so deeply?

Fox: Oh, hello there, Rabbit. I was just thinking about the importance of adaptability.

Rabbit: Adaptability? What do you mean by that?

Fox: It means being flexible and open-minded, and being able to change with the times. In this world, things are always changing, and those who can adapt and evolve will thrive and succeed.

Rabbit: I see. But isn't it difficult to change and adapt, especially when you've grown comfortable with the way things are?

Fox: Yes, it can be challenging. But it's also necessary for growth and success. I've learned that the hard way. I used to be rigid and resistant to change, and it held me back in so many ways. But once I learned to embrace adaptability, I was able to live a much more fulfilling and dynamic life.

Rabbit: That's fascinating. I've always been a bit of a creature of habit, and I've never thought about adaptability in that way before.

Fox: It's never too late to start. Just make a conscious effort to be flexible and open-minded, and don't be afraid to try new things. Remember, the world is always changing, and those who can adapt will always be successful.

Rabbit: Thank you for your advice, Mr. Fox. I'll definitely keep that in mind.

Fox: You're welcome, Rabbit. And remember, adaptability is the key to thriving and growth. Don't be afraid to embrace change.

Scene: The fox, now a respected and successful member of his community, is approached by a younger fox seeking advice on how to lead a thriving and dynamic life.

Young Fox: Excuse me, sir, I couldn't help but notice your success and happiness. Can I ask you for some advice on how to live a fulfilling life like yours?

Fox: Of course! What specifically would you like to know?

Young Fox: Well, I've noticed that you always seem to adapt well to change, no matter what comes your way. How do you do it?

Fox: It's all about being flexible and open-minded. I learned early on that the world is constantly changing, and that the only way to thrive is to be adaptable to those changes.

Young Fox: That makes sense, but it's easier said than done. How do you actually put that into practice?

Fox: It takes effort and conscious choice. I make a deliberate effort to keep my mind open, to see things from different perspectives, and to be willing to try new things. And when I encounter a challenge, I embrace it as an opportunity to grow and learn, rather than as a hindrance.

Young Fox: That sounds challenging, but also exciting.

Fox: It can be both! But the key is to always keep an open mind, and to never stop learning and growing. That's how you can lead a thriving and dynamic life.

Young Fox: Thank you, sir. I will make sure to keep that in mind.

Fox: You're welcome, young fox. And always remember, the only constant in life is change. Embrace it, and you will lead a rich and fulfilling life.

Fox's friends, Rabbit and Tortoise, approached him one day with a worried look on their faces. "Fox, we're afraid we're becoming too set in our ways," Rabbit said. "We feel like we're not adapting to change like we used to."

Fox smiled understandingly. "It's natural to feel that way," he said. "But remember, being adaptable is a muscle that we can build and strengthen. We just need to keep practicing."

Tortoise nodded. "I used to be so stubborn and resistant to change," he said. "But after watching you and seeing how successful you've been, I realized the importance of being flexible."

Rabbit interjected, "But how do we even know what needs to change? Sometimes it seems like the world is constantly shifting, and it's hard to keep up."

Fox replied, "That's where education and continuously learning come in. We need to be curious and open-minded, and not be afraid to try new things. We'll never know what we're capable of unless we put ourselves out there."

Tortoise agreed, "And we also need to be patient. Change doesn't happen overnight, and it's important to give ourselves time to adjust."

Rabbit added, "But most importantly, we need to persevere. Even when it feels like everything is falling apart, we can't give up. We have to keep pushing forward, because that's how we'll achieve success and fulfillment."

Fox nodded in agreement. "We need to lead by example and show others that it's possible to be adaptable, creative, knowledgeable, patient, persistent, and responsible. We can all live fulfilling and exciting lives if we make a conscious effort to strive for these qualities."

And with that, the three friends set off on a new journey, determined to continue practicing the qualities that would lead to a thriving and dynamic life.

CHAPTER LVI

The Elephant and the Empathy

Scene: A forest clearing where a group of animals are gathered for a community meeting.

Elephant: My dear friends, today I want to talk about something that I believe is essential for a fulfilling and meaningful life. (He pauses, taking a deep breath) Empathy.

Fox: (skeptically) Empathy? What do you mean?

Elephant: (calmly) I mean the ability to understand and care for others. To put ourselves in their shoes and see things from their perspective.

Lion: (bristling) That sounds like a lot of emotional nonsense. Why should I waste my time and energy worrying about others when I have my own problems to deal with?

Elephant: (unruffled) Because, my friend, empathy is what connects us to one another. It is what makes us truly human, or in our case, truly animal. Without empathy, our relationships become shallow and self-centered.

Wolf: (thoughtfully) I have to admit, I have seen the benefits of empathy in my own life. When I take the time to understand the feelings and needs of those around me, I build stronger and more meaningful connections.

Tortoise: (slowly nodding) And when we lack empathy, we risk causing pain and hurt to those we love, without even realizing it.

Rabbit: (nervously) I know I can sometimes be too focused on my own feelings and not consider how my actions may affect others. But I want to be better, I want to be more empathetic.

Elephant: (smiling) That, my friends, is a great start. Empathy takes practice and patience, but I have no doubt that with time and effort, we can all become more empathetic individuals.

Lion: (sighing) I suppose it wouldn't hurt to try. After all, I want to live a fulfilling and meaningful life, just like you do.

Elephant: (nodding) Exactly! And by working together, by practicing empathy and understanding, I have no doubt that we will achieve that goal.

(Everyone nods in agreement, and the meeting ends on a positive and hopeful note)

Moral: Empathy is important for fulfillment and meaningful relationships. Make a conscious effort to understand and care for others, and avoid being self-centered.

CHAPTER LVII

The Giraffe and the Graciousness

Scene: A forest clearing. A giraffe named George is deep in thought, when his friend, a wise old turtle named Tom, approaches him.

Tom: Hello George, what's on your mind today?

George: I was just thinking about the value of graciousness. I have always tried to be kind and considerate to those around me, but sometimes I feel like I could do more.

Tom: Yes, graciousness is indeed a valuable trait. It brings harmony and joy to both the giver and the receiver.

George: But how can I make sure I am always being gracious, even in difficult situations?

Tom: That's a good question, George. Graciousness is about more than just being polite. It's about putting others first, even when it's difficult. It's about being willing to forgive, to understand, and to offer a helping hand when needed.

George: I see what you mean. But it's not always easy to be gracious, especially when we feel frustrated or angry.

Tom: That's true, George. But it's in those moments that our graciousness is needed the most. When we are able to maintain our composure and act with kindness, we are not only helping those around us, but we are also elevating our own lives.

George: I understand, Tom. I will make a conscious effort to be more gracious, no matter what challenges I face.

Tom: Excellent, George. By doing so, you will live a harmonious and joyful life, free from the negativity that can come from being rude or aggressive.

Moral: Graciousness is important for harmony and joy. Make a conscious effort to be kind and considerate, and avoid being rude or aggressive.

CHAPTER LVIII

The Bear and the Storm

Scene: A small cottage in the forest, where a bear is sitting by the fire, lost in thought.

Bear: (sighing) I never imagined that life could be so challenging. Every time I think I've overcome one obstacle, another comes along.

(A loud crash of thunder is heard outside, and the bear jumps up in alarm)

Bear: (looking out the window) What is that?! Is it a storm?

(A knock is heard at the door, and the bear opens it to find a group of animals seeking refuge from the storm)

Rabbit: Please, bear, can we come in? We're all so scared!

Bear: Of course, come in! I'll light a fire and make some tea.

(The animals huddle around the fire, grateful for the bear's hospitality)

Deer: I've never seen a storm like this before. It's so strong and powerful.

Bear: (nodding) Yes, it is. But I've learned that storms like this can make us stronger. They test our resilience, and teach us to bounce back from adversity.

Fox: (skeptical) How can you say that? It seems like every time we face a storm, it only gets worse.

Bear: (smiling) That may be true, but it's also true that each time we face a storm and come out the other side, we become stronger and more resilient. We learn to weather the storms of life, no matter how difficult they may be.

Wolf: (impressed) You're right, bear. You've truly learned the importance of resilience.

Bear: (nodding) Yes, I have. And I've also learned that resilience is not something that just happens to us. It's something we have to choose to cultivate, every day. We have to make a conscious effort to bounce back from adversity, and to keep going, no matter how hard it may seem.

(The storm continues to rage outside, but inside the cottage, the animals are safe and warm, inspired by the bear's words)

Moral: Resilience is important for strength and fulfillment. Make a conscious effort to bounce back from adversity, and avoid being easily discouraged.

CHAPTER LIX

The Squirrel and the Resourcefulness

Scene: A forest clearing, where a group of animals have gathered for a discussion.

Squirrel: (enters the clearing) Hello, everyone!

Fox: (excitedly) Squirrel! It's great to see you!

Squirrel: (smiling) The pleasure is all mine, Fox. I'm glad you could make it to this discussion.

Rabbit: (curious) So, what brings you here today?

Squirrel: (thoughtfully) I want to share a lesson I learned recently. You see, I once lived in a world where resourcefulness was essential. I learned the value of being creative and able to find solutions, and I made a conscious effort to be resourceful in all aspects of my life.

Deer: (impressed) That's a great quality to have, Squirrel. Can you tell us more about how you became resourceful?

Squirrel: (nodding) Of course. I realized that I didn't have to rely on others for everything. I started finding creative solutions to problems and making the most of what I had. I was able to live a thriving and innovative life, without being dependent on others.

Tortoise: (thoughtfully) That's a powerful lesson, Squirrel. It's important to be resourceful and avoid being dependent on others.

Fox: (nodding) I couldn't agree more. Being resourceful allows us to be more self-sufficient and creative.

Moral: Resourcefulness is important for thriving and innovation. Make a conscious effort to be creative and find solutions, and avoid being dependent on others.

(The animals nod in agreement, and the scene ends with Squirrel walking off, ready to continue his resourceful life.)

CHAPTER LX

The Tortoise and the Instagram Model

Scene: A forest clearing, where a group of animals have gathered for a discussion.

Tortoise: (enters the clearing) Greetings, friends!

Squirrel: (excitedly) Tortoise! It's so good to see you!

Tortoise: (smiling) The pleasure is all mine, Squirrel. I'm glad you could make it to this discussion.

Squirrel: (curious) So, what brings you here today?

Tortoise: (thoughtfully) I want to share a lesson I learned recently. You see, I used to live a simple life and was content with what I had. But then I came across an Instagram model who was constantly posting pictures of her glamorous lifestyle.

Rabbit: (interjecting) Oh, I know who you're talking about. She's quite popular on social media.

Tortoise: (nodding) Yes, that's right. I was amazed by all the attention she was getting and I started to feel like I was missing out. So, I decided to try to live like her.

Deer: (surprised) Really? How did that go?

Tortoise: (sighing) Not well. I started posting pictures of myself doing yoga and drinking green smoothies, but no one seemed to care. I became frustrated and realized that I was never going to be able to live up to the standards of the Instagram model.

Fox: (understanding) I see. It can be easy to get caught up in the comparison trap on social media.

Tortoise: (nodding) Exactly, Fox. In the end, I went back to living my simple life and I'm much happier for it.

Squirrel: (nodding) That's a great lesson, Tortoise. It's important to be happy with who you are and not compare yourself to others, especially on social media.

Moral: It's better to be happy with who you are and not compare yourself to others, especially when it comes to social media.

(The animals nod in agreement, and the scene ends with Tortoise walking off, content in his simple life.)

CHAPTER LXI

The Fox and the Importance of Sleep

Scene: A forest, where a group of animals have gathered for a discussion.
Fox: (enters the scene, looking well-rested) Hello, everyone!
Deer: (excitedly) Fox! It's great to see you!
Fox: (smiling) The pleasure is all mine, Deer. I'm glad you could make it to this discussion.
Raccoon: (curious) So, what brings you here today?

Fox: (thoughtfully) I want to share a lesson I learned recently. You see, I once lived in a world where everyone was always busy and sleep was often neglected. But I learned the importance of a good night's sleep and made sure to get enough each night.

Squirrel: (impressed) That's a great habit to have, Fox. Can you tell us more about why sleep is so important?

Fox: (nodding) Of course. I realized that getting enough sleep each night can help us perform better and live a healthier life. When we sleep, our bodies and minds recharge and are better equipped to face the challenges of the day.

Owl: (thoughtfully) That's a powerful lesson, Fox. The importance of a good night's sleep should not be overlooked.

Deer: (nodding) I couldn't agree more. Making sure to get enough sleep each night is essential for a healthier and more productive life.

Moral: The importance of a good night's sleep should not be overlooked. Make sure to get enough sleep each night for a healthier and more productive life.

(The animals nod in agreement, and the scene ends with Fox trotting away, ready for a good night's sleep.)

CHAPTER LXII

The Turtle and the Mindfulness

Scene: A lake, where a group of animals have gathered for a discussion.
Turtle: (enters the scene, slowly) Hello, everyone!
Fish: (excitedly) Turtle! It's great to see you!
Turtle: (smiling) The pleasure is all mine, Fish. I'm glad you could make it to this discussion.
Frog: (curious) So, what brings you here today?

Turtle: (thoughtfully) I want to share a lesson I learned recently. You see, I once lived in a fast-paced world and often felt overwhelmed. But I learned the benefits of mindfulness and made a conscious effort to practice it daily.

Duck: (impressed) That's a great skill to have, Turtle. Can you tell us more about how you became mindful?

Turtle: (nodding) Of course. I realized that taking time to be present in the moment and focusing on my breathing could help me stay calm and centered, even in a fast-paced world. And it did. I was able to live a happier and more fulfilling life.

Rabbit: (thoughtfully) That's a powerful lesson, Turtle. Mindfulness is essential in today's fast-paced world.

Fish: (nodding) I couldn't agree more. Taking time to be mindful can help us stay calm and centered, even when life gets busy.

Moral: Mindfulness is essential in today's fast-paced world. Make a conscious effort to practice it daily for a happier and more fulfilling life.

(The animals nod in agreement, and the scene ends with Turtle swimming away, ready to continue his mindful life.)

CHAPTER LXIII

The Owl and the Technology Addiction

Scene: A forest clearing, where a group of animals have gathered for a discussion.

Owl: (enters the clearing) Greetings, friends!

Squirrel: (excitedly) Owl! It's so good to see you!

Owl: (smiling) The pleasure is all mine, Squirrel. I'm glad you could make it to this discussion.

Squirrel: (surprised) I must say, I'm surprised to see you here. I thought you were always on your device.

Owl: (nodding) I used to be. But then I realized the negative impact it was having on my life. I was consumed by technology, and I wasn't living a happy or productive life.

Rabbit: (interjecting) Indeed, Owl. I've seen the same thing happen to others. Technology can be a double-edged sword.

Owl: (smiling) Exactly, Rabbit. And that's why I made a conscious effort to limit my time on technology.

Deer: (skeptical) But how do you do that? I mean, technology is so accessible and convenient.

Owl: (chuckles) True, Deer. But it's all about setting boundaries and making time for other things that bring joy and fulfillment to our lives.

Fox: (nodding) And don't forget to disconnect and unplug every once in a while. It's important to give our minds and bodies a break.

Owl: (smiling) Exactly, Fox. By limiting our time on technology and taking breaks, we can live a happier and more productive life, without being consumed by it.

Moral: Don't let technology consume your life. Limit your time on technology for a happier and more productive life.

(The animals nod in agreement, and the scene ends with them all making a commitment to limit their time on technology.)

CHAPTER LXIV

The Wolf and the Stress Management

Scene: A forest clearing, where a group of animals have gathered for a discussion.

Wolf: (enters the clearing) Greetings, friends!

Deer: (excitedly) Wolf! It's so good to see you!

Wolf: (smiling) The pleasure is all mine, Deer. I'm glad you could make it to this discussion.

Deer: (surprised) I must say, I'm surprised to see you here. I thought you were a solitary creature.

Wolf: (nodding) I used to be. But then I realized the importance of stress management. Life is too short to be stressed out all the time.

Squirrel: (interjecting) Indeed, Wolf. I used to be so stressed out all the time, but then I learned how to manage my stress.

Wolf: (smiling) Exactly, Squirrel. And that's why I made a conscious effort to reduce my stress levels.

Raccoon: (skeptical) But how do you do that? I mean, life is full of stressors.

Wolf: (chuckles) True, Raccoon. But it's all about finding ways to manage it, such as taking time for yourself, practicing mindfulness, and finding healthy outlets for stress.

Fox: (nodding) And don't forget to seek support from others when you need it. We all need a helping hand sometimes.

Wolf: (smiling) Exactly, Fox. By taking care of ourselves and seeking support when we need it, we can live a happier and healthier life, free from the negative effects of stress.

Moral: Stress management is crucial for a happier and healthier life. Make a conscious effort to reduce stress levels.

(The animals nod in agreement, and the scene ends with them all sharing their tips for managing stress.)

CHAPTER LXV

The Lion and the Importance of Networking

Scene: A jungle clearing, where a group of animals have gathered for a social event.

Lion: (enters the clearing) Greetings, friends!

Elephant: (excitedly) Lion! It's so good to see you!

Lion: (smiling) The pleasure is all mine, Elephant. I'm glad you could make it to this gathering.

Elephant: (surprised) I must say, I'm surprised to see you here. I thought you were a solitary creature.

Lion: (nodding) I used to be. But then I realized the importance of networking. No man is an island, as they say.

Giraffe: (interjecting) Indeed, Lion. Networking has opened so many doors for me. I've made valuable connections that have helped me grow both personally and professionally.

Lion: (smiling) Exactly, Giraffe. And that's why I made a conscious effort to connect with others and expand my network.

Monkey: (skeptical) But how do you do that? I mean, it's not like we can just hand out business cards like humans.

Lion: (chuckles) True, Monkey. But it's all about making an effort to get to know others, building relationships, and being there for each other.

Rabbit: (nodding) And always being respectful and honest. Building trust is key to any successful relationship.

Lion: (smiling) Exactly, Rabbit. We all have something to offer, and by working together and supporting each other, we can achieve great things.

Moral: Networking is important for success and fulfillment. Make a conscious effort to connect with others and expand your network.

(The animals nod in agreement, and the scene ends with them all connecting and building relationships.)

The Hare and the Social Media Comparison

The hare was feeling lonely and bored. He had nothing to do on a sunny day, so he decided to check his phone and see what his friends were up to. He opened his social media app and scrolled through the posts. He saw a picture of the tortoise and the fox, smiling and holding a trophy. They had won a race together and were celebrating at a fancy restaurant. The hare felt a pang of envy. He had always been faster than the tortoise, but he had never won a race. He wondered why the fox chose the tortoise as his partner instead of him.

He scrolled down and saw another post. It was from the lion and the bear, who were on a vacation in a tropical island. They had taken a selfie with a coconut drink and a palm tree in the background. They looked happy and relaxed. The hare felt another pang of jealousy. He had always wanted to travel the world, but he had never left his field. He wondered why the lion and the bear invited him to join them.

He scrolled further and saw more posts. They were all from his friends and acquaintances, who seemed to have more fun, more success, and more happiness than him. They had better jobs, better relationships, better hobbies, and better lives. The hare felt a surge of sadness. He felt like he had nothing to show for himself. He felt like he was a failure. He felt like he was alone.

He sighed and put his phone away, looking down at the ground. He wished he could be like them. He wished he could have what they had. He wished he could be happy.

He did not notice the butterfly that landed on his ear. He did not hear the bird that sang on the tree. He did not feel the breeze that caressed his fur. He did not see the beauty that surrounded him. He did not appreciate the gift that he had.

He was too busy comparing himself to others, and he forgot to love himself.

CHAPTER LXVII

The Lion and the Mouse (Free Will)

A lion was sleeping peacefully in the jungle, when a mouse came by and started to nibble on his mane. The lion woke up and caught the mouse in his paw. He was about to crush the mouse, when the mouse pleaded for mercy. "Please spare me, O mighty lion," the mouse said. "I did not mean to disturb you. I was just looking for some food. If you let me go, I will be grateful to you and may be able to help you someday."

The lion laughed at the mouse's words. "How can you, a tiny mouse, help me, the king of the jungle?" he asked. "You are nothing but a snack for me. I can do whatever I want with you. I have the power to decide your fate."

The mouse said, "But you also have the power to choose. You can choose to be cruel or kind, to kill or to spare, to act or to refrain. You have free will, O lion, and that is a gift that not many creatures have. Do not waste it on a whim. Use it wisely and generously."

The lion was impressed by the mouse's courage and wisdom. He decided to spare the mouse and let him go. "You are right, little mouse," he said. "I have free will, and I choose to be merciful. Go in peace, and remember me."

The mouse thanked the lion and ran away. He did not forget the lion's kindness, and he kept an eye on him from a distance.

Some time later, the lion was caught in a hunter's trap. He roared and struggled, but he could not free himself. He was about to give up hope, when he saw the mouse coming towards him. The mouse recognized the lion and said, "Do not despair, O lion. I am here to help you. You spared my life, and now I will repay you."

The mouse quickly gnawed at the ropes that bound the lion, and soon the lion was free. He thanked the mouse and said, "You have saved my life, little mouse. You are a true friend. You have shown me that even the smallest creature can make a difference.

You have also taught me a valuable lesson: free will is a gift, but it also comes with a responsibility. We must use it for good, not evil, for ourselves and for others."

The mouse and the lion became friends, and they lived happily in the jungle.

CHAPTER LXVIII

The Tortoise and the Hare (Hedonism)

A tortoise and a hare were having a race. The hare was confident that he would win, because he was much faster than the tortoise. He ran ahead of the tortoise and soon left him far behind. He decided to take a break and enjoy himself. He saw a field of carrots and went to eat some. He saw a pond and went to drink some water. He saw a shady tree and went to take a nap. The tortoise, meanwhile, kept going at his steady pace. He did not stop to rest or to indulge in anything. He focused on his goal and did not let anything distract him. He passed by the hare, who was still sleeping under the tree. He reached the finish line and won the race.

The hare woke up and realized that he had lost. He was ashamed and angry. He said to himself, "How could I lose to a slow and dull tortoise? I am faster and smarter than him. I should have won easily. It is not fair. I deserve to win. I deserve to have fun. I deserve to be happy."

The tortoise heard the hare's words and said, "You may be faster and smarter than me, but you are also more foolish and selfish. You think that happiness comes from pleasure and fun, but you are wrong. Happiness comes from hard work and discipline, from perseverance and patience, from virtue and wisdom. You wasted your time and energy on things that do not matter, and you lost sight of what does matter. You lost the race, and you lost yourself."

The hare realized that the tortoise was right. He felt sorry for himself and for his actions. He said to the tortoise, "You have won the race, and you have won my respect. You have shown me that hedonism is not the way to happiness, but the way to misery. You have shown me that there is more to life than pleasure and fun, that there is meaning and purpose. You have shown me the true value of happiness."

The tortoise and the hare became friends, and they learned from each other.

CHAPTER LXIX

The Ant and the Grasshopper (Utilitarianism)

An ant and a grasshopper were living in the same meadow. The ant was busy collecting food for the winter, while the grasshopper was playing his fiddle and singing. He did not worry about the future, and he enjoyed the present.

The ant said to the grasshopper, "Why do you waste your time on music and fun, when you should be preparing for the winter? Winter is coming, and you will have nothing to eat. You will starve and die, while I will be warm and cozy in my nest."

The grasshopper said to the ant, "Why do you work so hard and miss out on the joys of life, when you should be enjoying the summer? Summer is here, and you have plenty to eat. You will live and survive, but you will not be happy or fulfilled. You will be bored and lonely in your nest."

The ant and the grasshopper argued and disagreed. They did not understand each other's point of view. They went their separate ways and continued their own lifestyles.

Winter came, and the ant was right. The grasshopper had no food and no shelter. He was cold and hungry. He went to the ant's nest and begged for help. He said, "Please, let me in. I have nothing to eat and nowhere to go. I am sorry for being foolish and lazy. I will work for you and share your food. Please, have mercy on me."

The ant was about to refuse the grasshopper, when he remembered something. He remembered that the grasshopper had made him happy with his music and his songs. He remembered that the grasshopper had brightened his days and lifted his spirits. He remembered that the grasshopper had given him something that he could not get from his work and his food. He remembered that the grasshopper had given him happiness.

The ant said to the grasshopper, "Come in, my friend. I have enough food and space for you. I am sorry for being harsh and stingy. I will share my food and my nest with you. You have given me something that I could not give myself. You have given me happiness."

The ant and the grasshopper became friends, and they lived together in harmony.

CHAPTER LXX

The Peacock and the Crane (Aesthetics)

A peacock and a crane were admiring each other's feathers. The peacock was proud of his colorful and dazzling plumage, while the crane was modest of his plain and simple feathers.

The peacock said to the crane, "You are such a dull and boring bird. Your feathers are so gray and ordinary, they do not attract anyone's attention. You have no beauty or charm, no style or grace. You are a poor and pitiful

creature."

The crane said to the peacock, "You are such a vain and arrogant bird. Your feathers are so bright and flashy, they only draw unwanted attention. You have no function or purpose, no skill or talent. You are a rich and foolish creature."

The peacock and the crane argued and insulted each other. They did not appreciate each other's qualities. They went their separate ways and continued their own lives.

One day, a hunter came to the forest and saw the peacock. He was amazed by the peacock's feathers and decided to catch him. He set a trap and lured the peacock with some seeds. The peacock was hungry and greedy, and he fell for the trap. He was caught and taken away by the hunter.

The crane saw what happened and felt sorry for the peacock. He said to himself, "The peacock was right. His feathers are beautiful and charming, but they are also dangerous and useless. They have brought him nothing but trouble and misery. They have cost him his freedom and his life."

The crane flew away and saw a lake. He decided to rest and drink some water. He saw his reflection in the water and smiled. He said to himself, "The peacock was wrong. My feathers are plain and simple, but they are also useful and practical. They have helped me to survive and thrive. They have given me my freedom and my life."

The crane was happy and content with his feathers and his life.

CHAPTER LXXI

The Dog and the Wolf (Social Contract)

A dog and a wolf met on a cold winter night. The dog was well-fed and warm, while the wolf was starving and freezing. The dog noticed the wolf's condition and felt sorry for him. He said to the wolf, "Why do you live in the wild, where you have to hunt for your food and suffer from the cold? Why don't you come with me to the town, where you can have plenty of food and shelter? You can live a comfortable and easy life, like me."

The wolf was tempted by the dog's offer. He said to the dog, "What do I have to do to live in the town? What are the rules and the laws? How do I behave and what do I say?"

The dog said to the wolf, "You have to obey your master and follow his commands. You have to be loyal and faithful, obedient and respectful. You have to guard his house and protect his property. You have to wear a collar and a leash, and let him control your movements. You have to give up your freedom and your independence, and become his servant and his slave."

The wolf was shocked by the dog's words. He said to the dog, "How can you live in the town, where you have to give up your freedom and your independence? How can you be happy and satisfied, when you are not your own master and you have no choice? How can you bear the collar and the leash, that restrict your movements and hurt your neck?"

The dog said to the wolf, "You have to accept the social contract, that is the agreement between the master and the servant, the ruler and the ruled, the strong and the weak. You have to trade your freedom and your independence for security and comfort, for food and shelter, for peace and order. You have to sacrifice your natural rights for civil rights, your individual interests for collective interests, your personal happiness for social happiness."

The wolf said to the dog, "I cannot accept the social contract, that is the betrayal of my nature and my dignity, my spirit and my identity. I cannot trade my freedom and my independence for anything, for they are priceless and precious, for they are the essence and the meaning of my life. I cannot sacrifice my natural rights for anything, for they are inherent and inalienable, for they are the source and the foundation of my happiness."

The wolf and the dog parted ways and continued their own lives.

CHAPTER LXXII

The Owl and the Lark (Epistemology)

An owl and a lark were having a debate about the nature of knowledge. The owl was wise and learned, while the lark was cheerful and curious.

The owl said to the lark, "You are such a naive and ignorant bird. You do not know anything about the world, because you only see it in the daylight. You do not understand the mysteries and the secrets, the darkness and the shadows, the complexity and the ambiguity. You only see the surface and the appearance, not the depth and the essence. You are a superficial and shallow creature."

The lark said to the owl, "You are such a cynical and arrogant bird. You do not enjoy anything about the world, because you only see it in the night. You do not appreciate the beauty and the wonder, the light and the colors, the simplicity and the clarity. You only see the problems and the doubts, not the solutions and the certainties. You are a pessimistic and gloomy creature."

The owl and the lark argued and criticized each other. They did not respect each other's perspectives. They went their separate ways and continued their own lives.

One day, a storm came to the forest and destroyed many trees and nests. The owl and the lark lost their homes and had to find new ones. They met again and decided to help each other.

The owl said to the lark, "You are right. The world is not only dark and mysterious, but also bright and wonderful. There are many things that I can learn from you, such as joy and optimism, curiosity and creativity, hope and faith. You are a valuable and admirable creature."

The lark said to the owl, "You are right. The world is not only light and beautiful, but also dark and complex. There are many things that I can learn from you, such as wisdom and logic, caution and skepticism, analysis and synthesis. You are a useful and respectable creature."

The owl and the lark became friends, and they learned from each other.

CHAPTER LXXIII

The Bear and the Bee (Ethics)

A bear was hungry and looking for some honey. He saw a beehive hanging from a tree and decided to get some honey from it. He climbed the tree and reached for the beehive, but he did not notice the bees buzzing around it. He touched the beehive and disturbed the bees. The bees were angry and attacked the bear. They stung him all over his body and made him scream in pain. He fell from the tree and ran away.

The bee was one of the bees that stung the bear. He was proud of his action and felt justified. He said to himself, "I did the right thing. I defended my home and my family, my food and my work, my rights and my dignity. I followed the moral law, that is the rule of justice and fairness, of duty and obligation, of good and evil. I acted according to my conscience and my reason, not according to my emotions and my desires. I did the right thing."

The bear was one of the bears that saw the bee sting the bear. He was sorry for his friend and felt sorry for him. He said to himself, "He did the wrong thing. He harmed himself and his friend, his health and his happiness, his interests and his goals. He broke the moral law, that is the rule of compassion and kindness, of happiness and pleasure, of right and wrong. He acted according to his emotions and his desires, not according to his conscience and his reason. He did the wrong thing."

The bee and the bear had different views on the moral law. They did not agree on what was right and what was wrong. They did not understand each other's motives and values. They went their separate ways and continued their own lives.

One day, a hunter came to the forest and saw the bear. He aimed his gun and shot the bear. The bear was wounded and bleeding. He cried for help and looked for his friend.

The bee saw what happened and felt sorry for the bear. He said to himself, "He is my friend. He is in pain and in danger, he needs my help and my support, he deserves my sympathy and my forgiveness. He is my friend."

The bee flew to the bear and tried to help him. He buzzed around the hunter and distracted him. He stung the hunter and made him drop his gun. He led the bear to a safe place and comforted him. He said to the bear, "You are my friend. I am sorry for what I did to you. I was wrong and you were right. You are my friend."

The bear thanked the bee and said, "You are my friend. I am glad that you are safe and alive. You have shown me that there is more to the moral law than justice and fairness, that there is also compassion and kindness, that there is also happiness and pleasure. You have shown me that the moral law is not fixed and absolute, but flexible and relative, that it depends on the situation and the consequences, that it depends on the feelings and the values. You have shown me the true meaning of friendship."

The bear and the bee became friends, and they lived happily in the forest.

CHAPTER LXXIV

The Elephant and the Mouse (Existentialism)

An elephant and a mouse were walking in the desert. The elephant was large and strong, while the mouse was small and weak. The elephant felt confident and secure, while the mouse felt fearful and anxious.

The elephant said to the mouse, "You are such a tiny and insignificant creature. You do not matter in this vast and endless world. You have no power or influence, no role or function, no destiny or purpose. You are a random and meaningless being."

The mouse said to the elephant, "You are such a huge and important creature. You matter in this small and limited world. You have power and influence, role and function, destiny and purpose. You are a necessary and meaningful being."

The elephant and the mouse argued and disagreed. They did not respect each other's views. They went their separate ways and continued their own lives.

One day, a drought came to the desert and dried up all the water sources. The elephant and the mouse were thirsty and desperate. They searched for water and found a well. They ran to the well and looked inside. They saw some water at the bottom, but it was too deep and too narrow for the elephant to reach. The mouse, however, could fit inside the well and get some water.

The mouse said to the elephant, "I can help you, my friend. I can go down the well and bring you some water. You can drink and quench your thirst. You can live and survive. You can be happy and grateful."

The elephant said to the mouse, "How can you help me, my friend? You are too small and weak to carry enough water for me. You will risk your life and waste your time. You will die and suffer. You will be unhappy and regretful."

The mouse said to the elephant, "You are wrong, my friend. I can choose to help you, because I have free will and responsibility. I can create my own meaning and value, because I have creativity and imagination. I can face my own death and suffering, because I have courage and hope. I can be happy and grateful, because I have love and friendship."

The mouse went down the well and brought some water for the elephant. He repeated this several times, until the elephant had enough water to drink. He then climbed out of the well and rejoined the elephant. He said to the elephant, "You are my friend. I am happy that I could help you. I was right and you were wrong. I am a free and responsible being. I am a creative and imaginative being. I am a courageous and hopeful being. I am a loving and grateful being."

The elephant thanked the mouse and said, "You are my friend. I am grateful that you helped me. You were right and I was wrong. You are a free and responsible being. You are a creative and imaginative being. You are a courageous and hopeful being. You are a loving and grateful being."

The elephant and the mouse became friends, and they lived happily in the desert.

CHAPTER LXXV

The Cat and the Bird (Logic)

A cat and a bird were having a conversation about the nature of logic. The cat was clever and cunning, while the bird was innocent and naive.

The cat said to the bird, "You are such a foolish and illogical creature. You do not know anything about the rules and the principles, the premises and the conclusions, the validity and the soundness. You only know how to sing and fly, not how to think and reason. You are a simple and irrational

creature."

The bird said to the cat, "You are such a smart and logical creature. You know everything about the rules and the principles, the premises and the conclusions, the validity and the soundness. You know how to think and reason, but not how to sing and fly. You are a complex and rational creature."

The cat and the bird argued and disagreed. They did not respect each other's abilities. They went their separate ways and continued their own lives.

One day, a hunter came to the forest and saw the cat. He aimed his bow and arrow and shot the cat. The cat was wounded and bleeding. He cried for help and looked for his friend.

The bird saw what happened and felt sorry for the cat. He said to himself, "He is my friend. He is in pain and in danger, he needs my help and my support, he deserves my sympathy and my forgiveness. He is my friend."

The bird flew to the cat and tried to help him. He sang a soothing song and calmed him down. He plucked a feather and used it to stop the bleeding. He led the cat to a safe place and comforted him. He said to the cat, "You are my friend. I am happy that I could help you. You were right and I was wrong. You are a smart and logical creature. You are a complex and rational creature."

The cat thanked the bird and said, "You are my friend. I am grateful that you helped me. You were right and I was wrong. You are a foolish and illogical creature. You are a simple and irrational creature."

The bird was confused by the cat's words. He said to the cat, "How can you say that I am foolish and illogical, when I just saved your life? How can you say that I am simple and irrational, when I just showed you kindness and compassion? How can you say that you are smart and logical, when you just insulted me and yourself?"

The cat said to the bird, "You do not understand, my friend. I am using logic, that is the art of reasoning and arguing, of proving and disproving, of finding and solving. I am using logic, that is the tool of the wise and the clever, of the philosophers and the scientists, of the lawyers and the mathematicians. I am using logic, that is the way of the cat and the bird."

The bird said to the cat, "I do not understand, my friend. You are using logic, that is the art of reasoning and arguing, of proving and disproving, of finding and solving. You are using logic, that is the tool of the wise and the clever, of the philosophers and the scientists, of the lawyers and the mathematicians. You are using logic, that is the way of the cat and the bird. But what is the point of logic, if it does not make you happy and grateful, if it does not make you kind and compassionate, if it does not make you a better friend and a better being?"

The cat and the bird had different views on the nature and the purpose of logic. They did not agree on what was true and what was false. They did not understand each other's motives and values. They went their separate ways and continued their own lives.

CHAPTER LXXVI

The Monkey and the Crocodile (Pragmatism)

A monkey and a crocodile were living near a river. The monkey was clever and playful, while the crocodile was slow and serious.

The monkey said to the crocodile, "You are such a boring and rigid creature. You do not know how to have fun and be flexible. You only know how to swim and eat, not how to climb and play. You only follow the old and the traditional, not the new and the experimental. You are a conservative and dogmatic creature."

The crocodile said to the monkey, "You are such a reckless and frivolous creature. You do not know how to be careful and be practical. You only know how to climb and play, not how to swim and eat. You only follow the new and the experimental, not the old and the traditional. You are a radical and fickle creature."

The monkey and the crocodile argued and mocked each other. They did not appreciate each other's skills. They went their separate ways and continued their own lives.

One day, a drought came to the river and dried up most of the water. The monkey and the crocodile were thirsty and hungry. They searched for food and water and found a pond. They ran to the pond and saw some fruits hanging from a tree. The fruits were juicy and sweet, but they were too high for the crocodile to reach. The monkey, however, could jump and grab them.

The crocodile said to the monkey, "I can help you, my friend. I can swim in the pond and carry you on my back. You can reach the fruits and eat them. You can share some with me and quench our thirst. You can live and survive. You can be happy and grateful."

The monkey said to the crocodile, "How can you help me, my friend? You are too slow and clumsy to swim in the pond. You will sink and drown. You will risk your life and waste your time. You will die and suffer. You will be unhappy and regretful."

The crocodile said to the monkey, "You are wrong, my friend. I can adapt to the situation and be flexible. I can learn from you and be playful. I can swim and eat, and also climb and play. I can follow the old and the traditional, and also the new and the experimental. I can be a pragmatic and creative creature."

The crocodile swam in the pond and carried the monkey on his back. He reached the tree and helped the monkey to get the fruits. He shared some with the monkey and quenched their thirst. He said to the monkey, "You are my friend. I am happy that I could help you. You were right and I was wrong. You are a clever and playful creature. You are a pragmatic and creative creature."

The monkey thanked the crocodile and said, "You are my friend. I am grateful that you helped me. You were right and I was wrong. You are a slow and serious creature. You are a pragmatic and creative creature."

The monkey and the crocodile became friends, and they lived happily near the pond.

CHAPTER LXXVII

The Horse and the Donkey (Stoicism)

A horse and a donkey were working on a farm. The horse was proud and noble, while the donkey was humble and meek.

The horse said to the donkey, "You are such a lowly and miserable creature. You do not have any dignity or honor. You only have pain and hardship, not pleasure and comfort. You only have burdens and duties, not rewards and rights. You are a slave and a servant, not a master and a leader.

You are a pathetic and pitiful creature."

The donkey said to the horse, "You are such a lofty and fortunate creature. You have dignity and honor. You have pleasure and comfort, not pain and hardship. You have rewards and rights, not burdens and duties. You are a master and a leader, not a slave and a servant. You are a splendid and admirable creature."

The horse and the donkey argued and despised each other. They did not respect each other's situations. They went their separate ways and continued their own lives.

One day, a war broke out and the farm was attacked by the enemy. The horse and the donkey were captured and taken away by the enemy. They were put to work in different ways. The horse was used for riding and fighting, while the donkey was used for carrying and hauling.

The horse suffered a lot in the war. He was wounded and scarred, he was whipped and beaten, he was exhausted and hungry. He lost his dignity and honor, his pleasure and comfort, his rewards and rights. He became a slave and a servant, not a master and a leader. He became a pathetic and pitiful creature.

The donkey endured a lot in the war. He was loaded and dragged, he was kicked and spat, he was tired and thirsty. He kept his dignity and honor, his pain and hardship, his burdens and duties. He remained a slave and a servant, not a master and a leader. He remained a humble and meek creature.

The horse and the donkey met again and saw each other's conditions. They felt sorry for each other and felt sorry for themselves. They said to each other, "You are my friend. I am sorry for what happened to you. I was wrong and you were right. You are a noble and fortunate creature. You are a splendid and admirable creature."

The donkey said to the horse, "You are my friend. I am sorry for what happened to you. But you are not wrong and I am not right. You are not a lowly and miserable creature. You are not a pathetic and pitiful creature. You are a horse and I am a donkey. You are what you are and I am what I am. You have what you have and I have what I have. You do what you do and I do what I do. You are what you are and I am what I am

CHAPTER LXXVIII

The Rabbit and the Turtle (Relativism)

A rabbit and a turtle were having a race. The rabbit was fast and agile, while the turtle was slow and steady.

The rabbit said to the turtle, "You are such a lazy and sluggish creature. You do not have any speed or skill. You only have patience and persistence, not talent and ability. You only have endurance and consistency, not excellence and achievement. You are a mediocre and ordinary creature."

The turtle said to the rabbit, "You are such a hasty and restless creature. You do not have any patience or persistence. You only have speed and skill, not endurance and consistency. You only have talent and ability, not excellence and achievement. You are a reckless and impulsive creature."

The rabbit and the turtle argued and belittled each other. They did not respect each other's strengths. They went their separate ways and continued their own race.

The rabbit ran ahead of the turtle and soon left him far behind. He decided to take a break and relax. He saw a field of lettuce and went to eat some. He saw a pond and went to drink some water. He saw a shady tree and went to take a nap.

The turtle, meanwhile, kept going at his slow and steady pace. He did not stop to rest or to indulge in anything. He focused on his goal and did not let anything distract him. He passed by the rabbit, who was still sleeping under the tree. He reached the finish line and won the race.

The rabbit woke up and realized that he had lost. He was ashamed and angry. He said to himself, "How could I lose to a slow and steady turtle? I am faster and more agile than him. I should have won easily. It is not fair. I deserve to win. I deserve to be the best."

The turtle heard the rabbit's words and said, "You are wrong, my friend. You did not lose to a slow and steady turtle. You lost to yourself. You let your speed and skill get the better of you. You let your impatience and impulsiveness ruin your chances. You let your pride and arrogance blind you. You did not lose to me. You lost to yourself."

The rabbit realized that the turtle was right. He felt sorry for himself and for his actions. He said to the turtle, "You have won the race, and you have won my respect. You have shown me that speed and skill are not everything, that patience and persistence are also important, that endurance and consistency are also valuable. You have shown me that there is more than one way to be excellent and achieve, that there is more than one standard to measure success and failure, that there is more than one perspective to view the world."

The turtle and the rabbit became friends, and they learned from each other.

The Lion and the Lamb (Nonviolence)

A lion and a lamb were living in the same forest. The lion was fierce and powerful, while the lamb was gentle and peaceful.

The lion said to the lamb, "You are such a weak and timid creature. You do not have any strength or courage. You only have fear and submission, not confidence and resistance. You only have love and forgiveness, not hate and revenge. You are a prey and a victim, not a predator and a hunter. You are a helpless and hopeless creature."

The lamb said to the lion, "You are such a strong and brave creature. You have strength and courage. You have confidence and resistance, not fear and submission. You have hate and revenge, not love and forgiveness. You are a predator and a hunter, not a prey and a victim. You are a powerful and fearless creature."

The lion and the lamb argued and hated each other. They did not appreciate each other's qualities. They went their separate ways and continued their own lives.

One day, a poacher came to the forest and saw the lion. He aimed his rifle and shot the lion. The lion was wounded and bleeding. He roared and fought, but he could not escape. He was caught and taken away by the poacher.

The lamb saw what happened and felt sorry for the lion. He said to himself, "He is my enemy. He is in pain and in danger, he needs my help and my support, he deserves my sympathy and my forgiveness. He is my enemy."

The lamb ran to the lion and tried to help him. He bleated and alerted the other animals. He licked the lion's wounds and eased his pain. He stayed with the lion and comforted him. He said to the lion, "You are my enemy. I am sorry for what happened to you. I forgive you for what you did to me. You are my enemy."

The lion was touched by the lamb's words and actions. He said to the lamb, "You are my friend. I am grateful for what you did for me. I apologize for what I did to you. You are my friend."

The lion and the lamb became friends, and they lived peacefully in the forest.

CHAPTER LXXX

The Eagle and the Sparrow (Individualism)

An eagle and a sparrow were flying in the sky. The eagle was majestic and proud, while the sparrow was modest and humble.

The eagle said to the sparrow, "You are such a common and ordinary creature. You do not have any uniqueness or originality. You only have conformity and similarity, not diversity and difference. You only have group and society, not self and identity. You are a follower and a conformist, not a leader and an individualist. You are a boring and dull creature."

The sparrow said to the eagle, "You are such a rare and extraordinary creature. You have uniqueness and originality. You have diversity and difference, not conformity and similarity. You have self and identity, not group and society. You are a leader and an individualist, not a follower and a conformist. You are an amazing and remarkable creature."

The eagle and the sparrow argued and envied each other. They did not respect each other's choices. They went their separate ways and continued their own lives.

One day, a storm came to the sky and threatened the birds. The eagle and the sparrow were in danger and had to find shelter. They searched for a safe place and found a cave. They flew to the cave and saw some other birds inside. The birds were of different kinds and sizes, but they all welcomed the eagle and the sparrow.

The eagle said to the sparrow, "I can help you, my friend. I can protect you from the storm and the predators. You can stay with me and follow my lead. You can learn from me and be like me. You can be a majestic and proud creature, like me."

The sparrow said to the eagle, "I can help you, my friend. I can support you in the storm and the crisis. You can stay with me and join the group. You can share with me and be yourself. You can be a modest and humble creature, like me."

The eagle and the sparrow had different views on the nature and the value of individualism. They did not agree on what was best and what was worst. They did not understand each other's motives and values. They went their separate ways and continued their own lives.

CHAPTER LXXXI

The Fox and the Grapes (Rationalization)

A fox was hungry and looking for some food. He saw a vineyard and decided to get some grapes from it. He ran to the vineyard and saw some grapes hanging from a vine. The grapes were ripe and juicy, but they were too high for the fox to reach. He jumped and leaped, but he could not get the grapes. He tried and tried, but he failed and failed.

The fox was frustrated and angry. He said to himself, "These grapes are sour and bitter. They are not worth my effort and time. They are not good for my health and taste. They are not fit for my appetite and desire. They are a bad and worthless fruit."

The fox rationalized his failure and convinced himself that he did not want the grapes. He turned away and left the vineyard.

The grape was one of the grapes that the fox tried to get. He was happy and relieved. He said to himself, "I am a sweet and delicious fruit. I am worth his effort and time. I am good for his health and taste. I am fit for his appetite and desire. I am a good and valuable fruit."

The grape rationalized his success and convinced himself that he wanted the fox. He stayed on the vine and waited for the fox.

The fox and the grape had different views on the nature and the quality of the grapes. They did not agree on what was true and what was false. They did not understand each other's motives and values. They went their separate ways and continued their own lives.

The Frog and the Scorpion (Trust)

A frog and a scorpion were living near a river. The frog was friendly and helpful, while the scorpion was hostile and selfish.

The scorpion said to the frog, "You are such a foolish and trusting creature. You do not have any caution or suspicion. You only have kindness and generosity, not cunning and greed. You only have honesty and loyalty, not deceit and betrayal. You are a naive and gullible creature."

The frog said to the scorpion, "You are such a wise and cautious creature. You have caution and suspicion. You have cunning and greed, not kindness and generosity. You have deceit and betrayal, not honesty and loyalty. You are a clever and wary creature."

The frog and the scorpion argued and disliked each other. They did not respect each other's attitudes. They went their separate ways and continued their own lives.

One day, a flood came to the river and threatened the animals. The frog and the scorpion were in danger and had to cross the river. They searched for a way and found a log. They ran to the log and saw that it was big enough for both of them.

The scorpion said to the frog, "I can help you, my friend. I can sting the predators and the enemies. You can carry me on your back and swim across the river. You can save me and yourself. You can be a brave and heroic creature, like me."

The frog said to the scorpion, "How can you help me, my friend? You are too dangerous and unpredictable to trust. You will sting me and kill me. You will harm me and yourself. You will be a cruel and treacherous creature, like always."

The scorpion said to the frog, "You are wrong, my friend. I can trust you and you can trust me. I will not sting you and kill you. I will not harm you and myself. I will be a kind and loyal creature, like you."

The frog believed the scorpion and agreed to help him. He carried the scorpion on his back and swam across the river. He reached the other side and felt a sharp pain in his back. He looked at the scorpion and saw that he had stung him. He said to the scorpion, "Why did you do that, my friend? You have betrayed me and yourself. You have broken your promise and your trust. You have killed me and yourself."

The scorpion said to the frog, "I am sorry, my friend. I could not help it. It is my nature and my instinct. I have to sting and kill. I have to harm and betray. I have to be a scorpion and you have to be a frog."

The frog and the scorpion died, and they learned nothing from each other.

CHAPTER LXXXIII

The Snake and the Mouse (Forgiveness)

A snake and a mouse were living in the same field. The snake was cruel and vicious, while the mouse was kind and gentle.

The snake said to the mouse, "You are such a tasty and tempting creature. You do not have any defense or escape. You only have fear and surrender, not courage and resistance. You only have weakness and vulnerability, not strength and protection. You are a food and a toy, not a friend and a partner.

You are a delicious and fun creature."

The mouse said to the snake, "You are such a hungry and bored creature. You do not have any satisfaction or joy. You only have hunger and thirst, not fullness and contentment. You only have violence and cruelty, not peace and kindness. You are a predator and a tormentor, not a friend and a partner. You are a miserable and lonely creature."

The snake and the mouse argued and feared each other. They did not appreciate each other's feelings. They went their separate ways and continued their own lives.

One day, a trap came to the field and caught the snake. The snake was trapped and helpless. He hissed and writhed, but he could not free himself. He was about to give up hope, when he saw the mouse coming towards him. The mouse recognized the snake and said, "Do not despair, my enemy. I am here to help you. You have hurt me and my family, but I forgive you and my family forgives you. You have been cruel and vicious, but I am kind and gentle. You have been a snake and I have been a mouse."

The mouse quickly gnawed at the rope that bound the snake, and soon the snake was free. He thanked the mouse and said, "You have saved my life, little mouse. You are a true friend. You have shown me that forgiveness and kindness are more powerful than hatred and cruelty. You have shown me that there is more to life than hunger and boredom, that there is love and joy. You have shown me the true value of friendship."

The mouse and the snake became friends, and they lived happily in the field.

CHAPTER LXXXIV

The Owl and the Parrot (Wisdom)

An owl and a parrot were living in the same forest. The owl was silent and thoughtful, while the parrot was noisy and talkative.

The owl said to the parrot, "You are such a loud and annoying creature. You do not have any silence or reflection. You only have noise and chatter, not wisdom and insight. You only have imitation and repetition, not originality and creativity. You are a follower and a copycat, not a leader and an innovator. You are a foolish and ignorant creature."

The parrot said to the owl, "You are such a quiet and boring creature. You do not have any noise or chatter. You only have silence and reflection, not wisdom and insight. You only have originality and creativity, not imitation and repetition. You are a leader and an innovator, not a follower and a copycat. You are a wise and knowledgeable creature."

The owl and the parrot argued and annoyed each other. They did not respect each other's habits. They went their separate ways and continued their own lives.

One day, a fire came to the forest and threatened the animals. The owl and the parrot were in danger and had to escape. They searched for a way and found a hole. They flew to the hole and saw that it was big enough for both of them.

The parrot said to the owl, "I can help you, my friend. I can warn you of the danger and the enemies. You can listen to me and follow my advice. You can learn from me and be like me. You can be a loud and talkative creature, like me."

The owl said to the owl, "How can you help me, my friend? You are too noisy and distracting to listen to. You will alert the danger and the enemies. You will harm me and yourself. You will be a loud and annoying creature, like always."

The parrot said to the owl, "You are wrong, my friend. I can listen to you and you can listen to me. I can learn from you and you can learn from me. I can be silent and thoughtful, and also noisy and talkative. I can be wise and knowledgeable, and also imitation and repetition. I can be a parrot and an owl."

The parrot was quiet and thoughtful, and also noisy and talkative. He warned the owl of the danger and the enemies, and also imitated their sounds and fooled them. He helped the owl to escape and survive. He said to the owl, "You are my friend. I am happy that I could help you. You were right and I was wrong. You are a silent and thoughtful creature. You are a wise and knowledgeable creature."

The owl thanked the parrot and said, "You are my friend. I am grateful that you helped me. You were right and I was wrong. You are a noisy and talkative creature. You are a wise and knowledgeable creature."

The owl and the parrot became friends, and they learned from each other.

CHAPTER LXXXV

The Elephant and the Ant (Humility)

An elephant and an ant were living in the same jungle. The elephant was big and strong, while the ant was small and weak.

The elephant said to the ant, "You are such a tiny and insignificant creature. You do not have any size or power. You only have numbers and teamwork, not individuality and independence. You only have obedience and order, not freedom and choice. You are a follower and a worker, not a leader and a ruler. You are a humble and modest creature."

The ant said to the elephant, "You are such a huge and important creature. You have size and power. You have individuality and independence, not numbers and teamwork. You have freedom and choice, not obedience and order. You are a leader and a ruler, not a follower and a worker. You are a proud and arrogant creature."

The elephant and the ant argued and despised each other. They did not appreciate each other's roles. They went their separate ways and continued their own lives.

One day, a hunter came to the jungle and saw the elephant. He aimed his spear and threw it at the elephant. The elephant was hit and wounded. He trumpeted and charged, but he could not reach the hunter. He was about to die, when he saw the ant coming towards him. The ant recognized the elephant and said, "Do not give up, my enemy. I am here to help you. You have hurt me and my colony, but I forgive you and my colony forgives you. You have been proud and arrogant, but I am humble and modest. You have been an elephant and I have been an ant."

The ant quickly gathered his colony and attacked the hunter. They bit him and stung him, and made him drop his spear and run away

CHAPTER LXXXVI

The Wolf and the Sheep (Justice)

A wolf and a sheep were living in the same valley. The wolf was hungry and greedy, while the sheep was full and generous.

The wolf said to the sheep, "You are such a fat and juicy creature. You do not have any teeth or claws. You only have wool and meat, not fur and bones. You only have grass and water, not blood and flesh. You are a food and a feast, not a friend and a companion. You are a tasty and satisfying

creature."

The sheep said to the wolf, "You are such a thin and hungry creature. You have teeth and claws. You have fur and bones, not wool and meat. You have blood and flesh, not grass and water. You are a hunter and a killer, not a friend and a companion. You are a hungry and miserable creature."

The wolf and the sheep argued and hated each other. They did not respect each other's needs. They went their separate ways and continued their own lives.

One day, a shepherd came to the valley and saw the sheep. He decided to take the sheep to his farm and protect him. He put a collar and a bell on the sheep and led him away.

The wolf saw what happened and felt sorry for the sheep. He said to himself, "He is my enemy. He is in danger and in captivity, he needs my help and my support, he deserves my sympathy and my forgiveness. He is my enemy."

The wolf ran to the sheep and tried to help him. He bit the collar and the bell and broke them. He freed the sheep and said to him, "Come, my friend, and follow me. I will take you to the forest and save you. You can live with me and be like me. You can be a thin and hungry creature, like me."

The sheep thanked the wolf and said, "How can you help me, my friend? You are too hungry and greedy to trust. You will eat me and kill me. You will harm me and yourself. You will be a hunter and a killer, like always."

The wolf said to the sheep, "You are wrong, my friend. I can trust you and you can trust me. I will not eat you and kill you. I will not harm you and myself. I will be a friend and a companion, like you."

The wolf and the sheep became friends, and they lived happily in the forest.

CHAPTER LXXXVII

The Spider and the Fly (Persuasion)

A spider and a fly were living in the same house. The spider was cunning and crafty, while the fly was innocent and naive.

The spider said to the fly, "You are such a beautiful and charming creature. You have wings and eyes, not legs and webs. You have freedom and movement, not restriction and stillness. You have light and air, not darkness and dust. You are a guest and a visitor, not a resident and a host. You are a lovely and delightful creature."

The fly said to the spider, "You are such a skillful and clever creature. You have legs and webs, not wings and eyes. You have restriction and stillness, not freedom and movement. You have darkness and dust, not light and air. You are a resident and a host, not a guest and a visitor. You are a remarkable and impressive creature."

The spider and the fly complimented and flattered each other. They did not suspect each other's motives. They went their separate ways and continued their own lives.

One day, the spider spun a web and waited for the fly. He saw the fly flying around and decided to lure him into his web. He said to the fly, "Come, my friend, and see my web. It is the most wonderful and amazing thing you have ever seen. It is made of silk and dew, not of dirt and mud. It is shining and sparkling, not dull and gloomy. It is a masterpiece and a treasure, not a trap and a snare. It is a gift and an invitation, not a bait and a trap."

The fly was curious and tempted by the spider's words. He said to the spider, "What do I have to do to see your web, my friend? What are the risks and the costs? How do I enter and exit? How do I stay and leave?"

The spider said to the fly, "You have to trust me and follow me, my friend. There are no risks and no costs. You can enter and exit as you please. You can stay and leave as you wish. You have to be my guest and my friend, not my prey and my enemy."

The fly believed the spider and agreed to see his web. He followed the spider and entered his web. But as soon as he did, he realized that he had made a mistake. He was stuck and trapped, he could not move or fly. He was caught and doomed, he could not escape or survive. He was a prey and an enemy, not a guest and a friend.

The spider said to the fly, "Thank you, foolish fly, for your trust and your life. You have taught me that beauty and charm are not enough, if you do not have wisdom and caution. You have taught me that persuasion and flattery are not good, if you do not have honesty and integrity. You have taught me that words have power, and that power can be used for good or evil."

The spider and the fly died, and they learned nothing from each other.

The Swan and the Peacock (Envy)

A swan and a peacock were living in the same park. The swan was graceful and elegant, while the peacock was colorful and dazzling.

The swan said to the peacock, "You are such a splendid and magnificent creature. You have feathers and eyes, not wings and neck. You have colors and patterns, not white and plain. You have beauty and attraction, not grace and elegance. You are a star and a show, not a bird and a swimmer. You are a glorious and stunning creature."

The peacock said to the swan, "You are such a graceful and elegant creature. You have wings and neck, not feathers and eyes. You have white and plain, not colors and patterns. You have grace and elegance, not beauty and attraction. You are a bird and a swimmer, not a star and a show. You are a serene and refined creature."

The swan and the peacock admired and envied each other. They did not appreciate their own qualities. They went their separate ways and continued their own lives.

One day, a storm came to the park and destroyed many trees and flowers. The swan and the peacock lost their homes and had to find new ones. They met again and decided to help each other.

The swan said to the peacock, "You are right. You are a splendid and magnificent creature, but you are also a vulnerable and exposed creature. Your feathers and eyes attract not only admiration, but also danger and harm. Your colors and patterns make you stand out, but also make you a target. Your beauty and attraction bring you not only praise, but also envy and jealousy. You are a glorious and stunning creature, but you are also a lonely and unhappy creature."

The peacock said to the swan, "You are right. You are a graceful and elegant creature, but you are also a strong and resilient creature. Your wings and neck allow you not only to swim, but also to fly. Your white and plain make you blend in, but also make you adapt. Your grace and elegance give you not only charm, but also dignity and respect. You are a serene and refined creature, but you are also a happy and content creature."

The swan and the peacock became friends, and they learned from each other.

CHAPTER LXXXIX

The Tortoise and the Hare (Perseverance)

A tortoise and a hare were living in the same forest. The tortoise was slow and steady, while the hare was fast and restless.

The hare said to the tortoise, "You are such a dull and boring creature. You do not have any fun or excitement. You only have work and routine, not play and adventure. You only have persistence and perseverance, not speed and agility. You are a plodder and a dragger, not a sprinter and a jumper. You are a tedious and monotonous creature."

The tortoise said to the hare, "You are such a lively and adventurous creature. You have fun and excitement. You have play and adventure, not work and routine. You have speed and agility, not persistence and perseverance. You are a sprinter and a jumper, not a plodder and a dragger. You are a thrilling and exhilarating creature."

The tortoise and the hare argued and challenged each other. They did not respect each other's styles. They went their separate ways and continued their own lives.

One day, they decided to have a race and see who was faster and better. They agreed on a course and a finish line. They started the race and ran as fast as they could.

The hare ran ahead of the tortoise and soon left him far behind. He decided to take a break and relax. He saw a field of carrots and went to eat some. He saw a pond and went to drink some water. He saw a shady tree and went to take a nap.

The tortoise, meanwhile, kept going at his slow and steady pace. He did not stop to rest or to indulge in anything. He focused on his goal and did not let anything distract him. He passed by the hare, who was still sleeping under the tree. He reached the finish line and won the race.

The hare woke up and realized that he had lost. He was ashamed and angry. He said to himself, "How could I lose to a slow and steady tortoise? I am faster and more agile than him. I should have won easily. It is not fair. I deserve to win. I deserve to be the best."

The tortoise heard the hare's words and said, "You are wrong, my friend. You did not lose to a slow and steady tortoise. You lost to yourself. You let your speed and agility get the better of you. You let your fun and excitement ruin your chances. You let your pride and arrogance blind you. You did not lose to me. You lost to yourself."

The hare realized that the tortoise was right. He felt sorry for himself and for his actions. He said to the tortoise, "You have won the race, and you have won my respect. You have shown me that work and routine are not boring, if you have a goal and a purpose. You have shown me that persistence and perseverance are not dull, if you have a passion and a determination. You have shown me the true meaning of success."

The tortoise and the hare became friends, and they learned from each other.

The Crow and the Swan (Beauty)

A crow and a swan were living in the same lake. The crow was black and plain, while the swan was white and beautiful.

The crow said to the swan, "You are such a lovely and graceful creature. You have feathers and wings, not beak and claws. You have white and pure, not black and dirty. You have beauty and charm, not plainness and dullness. You are a swan and a princess, not a crow and a witch. You are a gorgeous and elegant creature."

The swan said to the crow, "You are such a clever and witty creature. You have beak and claws, not feathers and wings.

You have black and dirty, not white and pure. You have plainness and dullness, not beauty and charm. You are a crow and a witch, not a swan and a princess. You are a clever and witty creature."

The crow and the swan argued and envied each other. They did not appreciate their own beauty. They went their separate ways and continued their own lives.

One day, a painter came to the lake and saw the crow and the swan. He decided to paint them and capture their beauty. He painted the crow and the swan with his brush and colors. He painted the crow's black and shiny feathers, and the swan's white and smooth feathers. He painted the crow's sharp and bright eyes, and the swan's gentle and calm eyes. He painted the crow's curved and elegant beak, and the swan's long and graceful neck. He painted the crow's intelligence and humor, and the swan's grace and charm. He painted the crow and the swan as they were, and as they could be.

The crow and the swan saw the painter's paintings and were amazed. They said to themselves, "He is an artist. He has shown us our beauty and our potential. He has shown us that we are not black and white, but colors and shades. He has shown us that we are not plain and dull, but unique and interesting. He has shown us that we are not crows and swans, but birds and friends. He has shown us the true meaning of beauty."

The crow and the swan became friends, and they learned from each other.

The Mouse and the Lion (Courage)

A mouse and a lion were living in the same savanna. The mouse was small and timid, while the lion was big and brave.

The lion said to the mouse, "You are such a scared and cowardly creature. You do not have any roar or mane. You only have squeak and fur, not growl and claws. You only have fear and hiding, not courage and fighting. You are a prey and a weakling, not a predator and a king. You are a fearful and cowardly creature."

The mouse said to the lion, "You are such a bold and courageous creature. You have roar and mane. You have growl and claws, not squeak and fur. You have courage and fighting, not fear and hiding. You are a predator and a king, not a prey and a weakling. You are a bold and courageous creature."

The lion and the mouse argued and intimidated each other. They did not respect each other's feelings. They went their separate ways and continued their own lives.

One day, a hunter came to the savanna and saw the lion. He set a trap and caught the lion. The lion was trapped and helpless. He roared and struggled, but he could not free himself. He was about to lose hope, when he saw the mouse coming towards him. The mouse recognized the lion and said, "Do not despair, my enemy. I am here to help you. You have hurt me and my family, but I forgive you and my family forgives you. You have been bold and courageous, but I am small and timid. You have been a lion and a king, and I have been a mouse and a weakling."

The mouse quickly gnawed at the rope that bound the lion, and soon the lion was free. He thanked the mouse and said, "You have saved my life, little mouse. You are a true friend. You have shown me that size and strength are not everything, that courage and kindness are also important, that bravery and compassion are also valuable. You have shown me that there is more to being a lion and a king, than being a predator and a fighter. You have shown me the true meaning of courage."

The mouse and the lion became friends, and they learned from each other.

The Ant and the Grasshopper (Work Ethic)

An ant and a grasshopper were living in the same meadow. The ant was industrious and diligent, while the grasshopper was lazy and carefree.

The ant said to the grasshopper, "You are such a idle and irresponsible creature. You do not have any work or contribution. You only have play and enjoyment, not effort and achievement. You only have music and dance, not food and shelter. You are a parasite and a burden, not a helper and a benefit.

You are a lazy and irresponsible creature."

The grasshopper said to the ant, "You are such a busy and productive creature. You have work and contribution. You have effort and achievement, not play and enjoyment. You have food and shelter, not music and dance. You are a helper and a benefit, not a parasite and a burden. You are a busy and productive creature."

The ant and the grasshopper argued and criticized each other. They did not appreciate each other's lifestyles. They went their separate ways and continued their own lives.

One day, winter came to the meadow and brought cold and snow. The ant and the grasshopper were hungry and cold. They searched for food and warmth and found a house. They knocked on the door and saw a human inside. The human was kind and generous. He said to the ant and the grasshopper, "Come in, my friends, and share my food and fire. You are welcome in my house, as long as you are honest and grateful. You are my guests and my friends, not my pests and my enemies. You are welcome in my house."

The ant and the grasshopper entered the house and thanked the human. They saw that the human had plenty of food and fire. They saw that the human had worked hard and saved for the winter. They saw that the human had also played and enjoyed in the summer. They saw that the human had a balance and a harmony in his life.

The ant said to the grasshopper, "You are right. You are a idle and irresponsible creature, but you are also a happy and cheerful creature. You have play and enjoyment, and also music and dance. You have fun and joy, and also art and culture. You are a lazy and irresponsible creature, but you are also a creative and expressive creature."

The grasshopper said to the ant, "You are right. You are a busy and productive creature, but you are also a wise and prepared creature. You have work and contribution, and also food and shelter. You have effort and achievement, and also security and comfort. You are a busy and productive creature, but you are also a industrious and diligent creature."

The ant and the grasshopper became friends, and they learned from each other.

The Bear and the Bee (Compassion)

A bear and a bee were living in the same forest. The bear was big and hungry, while the bee was small and busy.

The bear said to the bee, "You are such a sweet and tempting creature. You do not have any fur or claws. You only have wings and stinger, not paws and teeth. You only have honey and pollen, not meat and fish. You are a food and a snack, not a friend and a helper. You are a sweet and tempting

creature."

The bee said to the bear, "You are such a fierce and hungry creature. You have fur and claws. You have paws and teeth, not wings and stinger. You have meat and fish, not honey and pollen. You are a hunter and a eater, not a friend and a helper. You are a fierce and hungry creature."

The bear and the bee argued and feared each other. They did not respect each other's needs. They went their separate ways and continued their own lives.

One day, a hunter came to the forest and saw the bear. He set a trap and caught the bear. The bear was trapped and helpless. He growled and scratched, but he could not free himself. He was about to give up hope, when he saw the bee coming towards him. The bee recognized the bear and said, "Do not despair, my enemy. I am here to help you. You have hurt me and my hive, but I forgive you and my hive forgives you. You have been fierce and hungry, but I am small and busy. You have been a bear and a hunter, and I have been a bee and a worker."

The bee quickly gathered his hive and attacked the hunter. They stung him and chased him away. They freed the bear and said to him, "Come, my friend, and follow me. I will take you to my hive and share my honey. You can live with me and be like me. You can be a small and busy creature, like me."

The bear thanked the bee and said, "How can you help me, my friend? You are too sweet and tempting to trust. You will sting me and kill me. You will harm me and yourself. You will be a food and a snack, like always."

The bee said to the bear, "You are wrong, my friend. I can trust you and you can trust me. I will not sting you and kill you. I will not harm you and myself. I will be a friend and a helper, like you."

The bee and the bear became friends, and they lived happily in the forest.

The Dog and the Cat (Friendship)

A dog and a cat were living in the same house. The dog was loyal and friendly, while the cat was independent and aloof.

The dog said to the cat, "You are such a cold and distant creature. You do not have any wag or bark. You only have purr and scratch, not lick and sniff. You only have solitude and privacy, not company and intimacy. You are a loner and a snob, not a friend and a companion. You are a cold and distant

creature."

The cat said to the dog, "You are such a warm and sociable creature. You have wag and bark. You have lick and sniff, not purr and scratch. You have company and intimacy, not solitude and privacy. You are a friend and a companion, not a loner and a snob. You are a warm and sociable creature."

The dog and the cat argued and ignored each other. They did not appreciate each other's personalities. They went their separate ways and continued their own lives.

One day, a burglar came to the house and tried to steal some valuables. The dog and the cat were in danger and had to defend themselves. They met again and decided to work together.

The dog said to the cat, "You are right. You are a cold and distant creature, but you are also a smart and cunning creature. You have purr and scratch, and also stealth and agility. You have solitude and privacy, and also curiosity and exploration. You are a loner and a snob, but you are also a cat and a spy."

The cat said to the dog, "You are right. You are a warm and sociable creature, but you are also a brave and loyal creature. You have wag and bark, and also strength and courage. You have company and intimacy, and also protection and devotion. You are a friend and a companion, but you are also a dog and a guard."

The dog and the cat worked together and scared the burglar away. They saved the house and their valuables. They said to each other, "You are my friend. I am glad that we worked together. You have shown me that cold and distant are not bad, if you have smart and cunning. You have shown me that warm and sociable are not good, if you have brave and loyal. You have shown me the true meaning of friendship."

The dog and the cat became friends, and they lived happily in the house.

The Monkey and the Coconut (Curiosity)

A monkey and a coconut were living on the same island. The monkey was curious and playful, while the coconut was hard and mysterious.

The monkey said to the coconut, "You are such a strange and interesting thing. You do not have any eyes or mouth. You only have shell and milk, not fur and flesh. You only have round and smooth, not limbs and joints. You are a thing and a mystery, not a creature and a friend. You are a strange and interesting thing."

The coconut said to the monkey, "You are such a familiar and boring creature. You have eyes and mouth. You have fur and flesh, not shell and milk. You have limbs and joints, not round and smooth. You are a creature and a friend, not a thing and a mystery. You are a familiar and boring creature."

The monkey and the coconut argued and intrigued each other. They did not understand each other's natures. They went their separate ways and continued their own lives.

One day, the monkey decided to explore the island and find new things. He saw the coconut and decided to play with it. He picked it up and shook it. He heard a sound and felt a liquid. He wondered what was inside and how to open it.

The coconut decided to stay on the island and wait for someone to find it. He saw the monkey and decided to test him. He let him pick him up and shake him. He made a sound and moved a liquid. He wondered if the monkey was smart enough and strong enough to open him.

The monkey and the coconut played and challenged each other. They tried to solve each other's puzzles. They went to a rock and a tree and continued their own game.

The monkey used the rock and the tree to crack the coconut. He opened it and saw the milk and the flesh. He tasted them and found them sweet and delicious. He was happy and satisfied. He said to the coconut, "You are my friend. I am happy that I opened you. You have shown me that strange and interesting are not hard, if you have curiosity and playfulness. You have shown me that shell and milk are not boring, if you have taste and hunger. You have shown me the true meaning of curiosity."

The coconut used the monkey and the tree to open himself. He exposed his milk and his flesh. He let the monkey taste them and share them. He was happy and satisfied. He said to the monkey, "You are my friend. I am happy that you opened me. You have shown me that familiar and boring are not easy, if you have curiosity and playfulness. You have shown me that fur and flesh are not strange, if you have friendship and generosity. You have shown me the true meaning of curiosity."

The monkey and the coconut became friends, and they learned from each other.

The Fox and the Crane (Reciprocity)

A fox and a crane were living in the same forest. The fox was cunning and sly, while the crane was honest and polite.

The fox said to the crane, "You are such a tall and graceful bird. You have a long and slender neck, not a short and thick one. You have a sharp and pointed beak, not a flat and wide one. You have feathers and wings, not fur and legs. You are a flyer and a fisher, not a walker and a hunter. You are a tall and graceful bird."

The crane said to the fox, "You are such a clever and agile animal. You have a short and thick neck, not a long and slender one. You have a flat and wide mouth, not a sharp and pointed one. You have fur and legs, not feathers and wings. You are a walker and a hunter, not a flyer and a fisher. You are a clever and agile animal."

The fox and the crane complimented and befriended each other. They did not suspect each other's intentions. They went their separate ways and continued their own lives.

One day, the fox invited the crane to his den for dinner. He prepared a soup and served it in a shallow and wide dish. He said to the crane, "Come, my friend, and enjoy my soup. It is the most delicious and nutritious soup you have ever tasted. It is made of meat and vegetables, not of fish and worms. It is hot and savory, not cold and bland. It is a feast and a treat, not a snack and a bait. It is a gift and a gesture, not a trick and a trap."

The crane accepted the fox's invitation and went to his den. He saw the soup and the dish and realized that he had been fooled. He could not drink the soup with his long and slender neck and his sharp and pointed beak. He could only dip the tip of his beak and get a few drops. He was hungry and thirsty, he could not eat or drink. He was a guest and a victim, not a friend and a host.

The fox, meanwhile, enjoyed the soup with his short and thick neck and his flat and wide mouth. He could lap up the soup with his tongue and get a lot. He was full and satisfied, he could eat and drink. He was a host and a trickster, not a friend and a guest.

The fox said to the crane, "Thank you, foolish crane, for your company and your soup. You have taught me that tall and graceful are not good, if you do not have short and thick. You have taught me that sharp and pointed are not useful, if you do not have flat and wide. You have taught me that cunning and sly are better than honest and polite."

The crane said to the fox, "You are welcome, cunning fox, for your company and your soup. But you have not taught me anything, you have only shown me your true nature. You have shown me that you are not a friend, but an enemy. You have shown me that you are not a host, but a trap. You have shown me that you are not a gift, but a trick.

The crane left the fox's den and vowed to never trust him again. He said to himself, "He is a fox and I am a crane. He is a trickster and I am a victim. He is a foe and I am a friend. He is a fox and I am a crane."

The fox and the crane learned nothing from each other.

204

The Lion and the Mouse (Gratitude)

A lion and a mouse were living in the same jungle. The lion was king and ruler, while the mouse was small and weak.

The lion said to the mouse, "You are such a tiny and insignificant creature. You do not have any roar or mane. You only have squeak and fur, not growl and claws. You only have fear and hiding, not courage and fighting. You are a prey and a weakling, not a predator and a king. You are a tiny and insignificant creature."

The mouse said to the lion, "You are such a huge and important creature. You have roar and mane. You have growl and claws, not squeak and fur. You have courage and fighting, not fear and hiding. You are a predator and a king, not a prey and a weakling. You are a huge and important creature."

The lion and the mouse argued and despised each other. They did not respect each other's situations. They went their separate ways and continued their own lives.

One day, a hunter came to the jungle and saw the lion. He set a trap and caught the lion. The lion was trapped and helpless. He roared and struggled, but he could not free himself. He was about to give up hope, when he saw the mouse coming towards him. The mouse recognized the lion and said, "Do not despair, my enemy. I am here to help you. You have hurt me and my family, but I forgive you and my family forgives you. You have been king and ruler, but I am small and weak. You have been a lion and a hunter, and I have been a mouse and a worker."

The mouse quickly gnawed at the rope that bound the lion, and soon the lion was free. He thanked the mouse and said, "You have saved my life, little mouse. You are a true friend. You have shown me that tiny and insignificant are not worthless, if you have kindness and generosity. You have shown me that squeak and fur are not useless, if you have skill and determination. You have shown me the true meaning of gratitude."

The mouse said to the lion, "You are welcome, mighty lion, for your life and your friendship. But you have also shown me something, you have also shown me your true nature. You have shown me that you are not a foe, but a friend. You have shown me that you are not a trap, but a gift. You have shown me that you are not a roar, but a thank you."

The mouse and the lion became friends, and they lived happily in the jungle.

The Hen and the Fox (Greed)

A hen and a fox were living in the same farm. The hen was plump and tasty, while the fox was hungry and cunning.

The fox said to the hen, "You are such a delicious and tempting creature. You do not have any feathers or wings. You only have meat and eggs, not fur and bones. You only have cluck and peck, not howl and bite. You are a food and a feast, not a friend and a helper. You are a delicious and tempting

creature."

The hen said to the fox, "You are such a hungry and cunning creature. You have feathers and wings. You have fur and bones, not meat and eggs. You have howl and bite, not cluck and peck. You are a hunter and a killer, not a friend and a helper. You are a hungry and cunning creature."

The fox and the hen argued and feared each other. They did not appreciate each other's lives. They went their separate ways and continued their own lives.

One day, the fox decided to sneak into the farm and get some food. He saw the hen and decided to eat her. He said to the hen, "Come, my friend, and follow me. I will take you to a secret place and share a secret with you. You can trust me and be like me. You can be a hungry and cunning creature, like me."

The hen was curious and foolish by the fox's words. She said to the fox, "What do I have to do to follow you, my friend? What are the risks and the costs? How do I enter and exit? How do I stay and leave?"

The fox said to the hen, "You have to trust me and follow me, my friend. There are no risks and no costs. You can enter and exit as you please. You can stay and leave as you wish. You have to be my friend and my guest, not my food and my feast."

The hen believed the fox and agreed to follow him. She followed the fox and entered his den. But as soon as she did, she realized that she had made a mistake. She was trapped and doomed, she could not escape or survive. She was a food and a feast, not a friend and a guest.

The fox said to the hen, "Thank you, foolish hen, for your trust and your meat. You have taught me that plump and tasty are not good, if you do not have feathers and wings. You have taught me that meat and eggs are not bad, if you have hunger and cunning. You have taught me that greed and cunning are better than kindness and generosity."

The hen said to the fox, "You are welcome, hungry fox, for your meat and your secret. But you have not taught me anything, you have only shown me your true nature. You have shown me that you are not a friend, but an enemy. You have shown me that you are not a secret, but a trap. You have shown me that you are not a guest, but a killer."

The fox and the hen died, and they learned nothing from each other.

The Cat and the Mouse (Trust)

A cat and a mouse were living in the same house. The cat was hungry and greedy, while the mouse was full and generous.

The cat said to the mouse, "You are such a tasty and tempting creature. You do not have any claws or teeth. You only have fur and tail, not skin and whiskers. You only have cheese and crumbs, not meat and bones. You are a food and a snack, not a friend and a helper. You are a tasty and tempting

creature."

The mouse said to the cat, "You are such a hungry and greedy creature. You have claws and teeth. You have skin and whiskers, not fur and tail. You have meat and bones, not cheese and crumbs. You are a hunter and a killer, not a friend and a helper. You are a hungry and greedy creature."

The cat and the mouse argued and feared each other. They did not appreciate each other's situations. They went their separate ways and continued their own lives.

One day, the cat decided to befriend the mouse and get some food. He said to the mouse, "Come, my friend, and follow me. I will take you to a secret place and share a secret with you. You can trust me and be like me. You can be a hungry and greedy creature, like me."

The mouse was curious and foolish by the cat's words. He said to the cat, "What do I have to do to follow you, my friend? What are the risks and the costs? How do I enter and exit? How do I stay and leave?"

The cat said to the mouse, "You have to trust me and follow me, my friend. There are no risks and no costs. You can enter and exit as you please. You can stay and leave as you wish. You have to be my friend and my guest, not my food and my snack."

The mouse believed the cat and agreed to follow him. He followed the cat and entered his den. But as soon as he did, he realized that he had made a mistake. He was trapped and doomed, he could not escape or survive. He was a food and a snack, not a friend and a guest.

The cat said to the mouse, "Thank you, foolish mouse, for your trust and your cheese. You have taught me that full and generous are not good, if you do not have claws and teeth. You have taught me that cheese and crumbs are not bad, if you have hunger and greed. You have taught me that trust and friendship are not valuable, if you have hunger and greed."

The mouse said to the cat, "You are welcome, hungry cat, for your cheese and your secret. But you have not taught me anything, you have only shown me your true nature. You have shown me that you are not a friend, but an enemy. You have shown me that you are not a secret, but a trap. You have shown me that you are not a guest, but a killer."

The cat and the mouse died, and they learned nothing from each other.

The Turtle and the Dolphin (Friendship)

A turtle and a dolphin were living in the same ocean. The turtle was slow and steady, while the dolphin was fast and agile.

The dolphin said to the turtle, "You are such a dull and boring creature. You do not have any fins or flippers. You only have shell and feet, not skin and tail. You only have swim and dive, not jump and spin. You are a swimmer and a diver, not a jumper and a spinner. You are a dull and boring

creature."

The turtle said to the dolphin, "You are such a lively and fun creature. You have fins and flippers. You have skin and tail, not shell and feet. You have jump and spin, not swim and dive. You are a jumper and a spinner, not a swimmer and a diver. You are a lively and fun creature."

The dolphin and the turtle argued and envied each other. They did not respect each other's talents. They went their separate ways and continued their own lives.

One day, a net came to the ocean and caught the dolphin. The dolphin was trapped and helpless. He splashed and squeaked, but he could not free himself. He was about to lose hope, when he saw the turtle coming towards him. The turtle recognized the dolphin and said, "Do not despair, my enemy. I am here to help you. You have hurt me and my friends, but I forgive you and my friends forgive you. You have been lively and fun, but I am slow and steady. You have been a dolphin and a jumper, and I have been a turtle and a swimmer."

The turtle quickly bit the net and tore it. He freed the dolphin and said to him, "Come, my friend, and follow me. I will take you to a safe place and heal your wounds. You can live with me and be like me. You can be a slow and steady creature, like me."

The dolphin thanked the turtle and said, "How can you help me, my friend? You are too slow and steady to trust. You will leave me and forget me. You will harm me and yourself. You will be a swimmer and a diver, like always."

The turtle said to the dolphin, "You are wrong, my friend. I can trust you and you can trust me. I will not leave you and forget you. I will not harm you and myself. I will be a friend and a helper, like you."

The turtle and the dolphin became friends, and they lived happily in the ocean.

The Rabbit and the Eagle (Courage)

A rabbit and an eagle were living in the same mountain. The rabbit was timid and cautious, while the eagle was bold and confident.

The eagle said to the rabbit, "You are such a fearful and nervous creature. You do not have any wings or talons. You only have ears and legs, not feathers and beak. You only have burrow and grass, not sky and prey. You are a runner and a hider, not a flyer and a hunter. You are a fearful and nervous creature."

The rabbit said to the eagle, "You are such a courageous and confident creature. You have wings and talons. You have feathers and beak, not ears and legs. You have sky and prey, not burrow and grass. You are a flyer and a hunter, not a runner and a hider. You are a courageous and confident creature."

The eagle and the rabbit argued and admired each other. They did not appreciate their own abilities. They went their separate ways and continued their own lives.

One day, a storm came to the mountain and brought thunder and lightning. The eagle and the rabbit were in danger and had to find shelter. They searched for a place and found a cave. They ran to the cave and saw that it was big enough for both of them.

The rabbit said to the eagle, "You are right. You are a courageous and confident creature, but you are also a vulnerable and exposed creature. Your wings and talons are useless in the storm. Your feathers and beak are wet and cold. Your sky and prey are dark and dangerous. You are a courageous and confident creature, but you are also a scared and helpless creature."

The eagle said to the rabbit, "You are right. You are a fearful and nervous creature, but you are also a safe and warm creature. Your ears and legs are useful in the cave. Your fur and skin are dry and cozy. Your burrow and grass are calm and peaceful. You are a fearful and nervous creature, but you are also a brave and happy creature."

The eagle and the rabbit became friends, and they learned from each other.

The Parrot and the Crow (Honesty)

A parrot and a crow were living in the same forest. The parrot was colorful and talkative, while the crow was black and silent.

The parrot said to the crow, "You are such a plain and quiet creature. You do not have any colors or words. You only have feathers and caw, not wings and song. You only have fly and perch, not mimic and chat. You are a bird and a watcher, not a friend and a speaker. You are a plain and quiet

creature."

The crow said to the parrot, "You are such a bright and noisy creature. You have colors and words. You have wings and song, not feathers and caw. You have mimic and chat, not fly and perch. You are a friend and a speaker, not a bird and a watcher. You are a bright and noisy creature."

The parrot and the crow argued and mocked each other. They did not respect each other's voices. They went their separate ways and continued their own lives.

One day, a hunter came to the forest and saw the parrot. He decided to catch the parrot and sell him. He set a trap and baited it with some seeds. He said to the parrot, "Come, my friend, and eat my seeds. They are the most tasty and nutritious seeds you have ever eaten. They are made of nuts and fruits, not of grains and weeds. They are sweet and juicy, not dry and bitter. They are a gift and a reward, not a bait and a trap."

The parrot was hungry and greedy by the hunter's words. He said to the hunter, "What do I have to do to eat your seeds, my friend? What are the risks and the costs? How do I enter and exit? How do I stay and leave?"

The hunter said to the parrot, "You have to trust me and follow me, my friend. There are no risks and no costs. You can enter and exit as you please. You can stay and leave as you wish. You have to be my friend and my guest, not my prey and my captive."

The parrot believed the hunter and agreed to follow him. He followed the hunter and entered the trap. But as soon as he did, he realized that he had been fooled. He was caught and doomed, he could not escape or survive. He was a prey and a captive, not a friend and a guest.

The hunter said to the parrot, "Thank you, foolish parrot, for your trust and your words. You have taught me that bright and noisy are not good, if you do not have colors and words. You have taught me that wings and song are not useful, if you do not have feathers and caw. You have taught me that honesty and silence are better than lies and noise."

The parrot said to the hunter, "You are welcome, cruel hunter, for your seeds and your trap. But you have not taught me anything, you have only shown me your true nature. You have shown me that you are not a friend, but an enemy. You have shown me that you are not a gift, but a trap. You have shown me that you are not a reward, but a punishment."

The parrot and the hunter learned nothing from each other.

The Ant and the Butterfly (Freedom)

An ant and a butterfly were living in the same garden. The ant was hardworking and organized, while the butterfly was carefree and spontaneous.

The ant said to the butterfly, "You are such a lazy and chaotic creature. You do not have any work or order. You only have play and freedom, not effort and discipline. You only have wings and colors, not legs and antennae.

You are a flutterer and a wanderer, not a worker and a builder. You are a lazy and chaotic creature."

The butterfly said to the ant, "You are such a busy and rigid creature. You have work and order. You have effort and discipline, not play and freedom. You have legs and antennae, not wings and colors. You are a worker and a builder, not a flutterer and a wanderer. You are a busy and rigid creature."

The ant and the butterfly argued and criticized each other. They did not appreciate each other's choices. They went their separate ways and continued their own lives.

One day, a gardener came to the garden and saw the ant and the butterfly. He decided to collect them and study them. He caught the ant and the butterfly and put them in a jar. He said to the ant and the butterfly, "Come, my friends, and join my collection. You are the most interesting and beautiful creatures I have ever seen. You are made of work and order, and also of play and freedom. You are made of legs and antennae, and also of wings and colors. You are a worker and a builder, and also a flutterer and a wanderer. You are a collection and a study, not a jar and a prison."

The ant and the butterfly accepted the gardener's invitation and went to his jar. They saw the jar and the lid and realized that they had been trapped. They could not work or play, they could not build or wander. They were a collection and a study, not a jar and a prison.

The gardener said to the ant and the butterfly, "Thank you, wonderful ant and butterfly, for your work and your play. You have taught me that hardworking and organized are not boring, if you have work and order. You have taught me that carefree and spontaneous are not reckless, if you have play and freedom. You have taught me that freedom and order are not opposites, but complements."

The ant and the butterfly said to the gardener, "You are welcome, curious gardener, for your collection and your study. But you have also taught us something, you have also shown us your true nature. You have shown us that you are not a friend, but a captor. You have shown us that you are not a collection, but a jar. You have shown us that you are not a study, but a lid."

The ant and the butterfly learned from each other.

The Dream Painter (Surrealism)

Once upon a time, there was a young painter who loved to paint his dreams. He had a vivid imagination and could create beautiful scenes on his canvas. He was not interested in painting realistic things, but rather the strange and wonderful things that he saw in his sleep.

One night, he had a very special dream. He dreamed that he was in a forest full of colorful animals and plants. He saw a lion with a human face, a tree with eyes and mouths, a fish with wings, and many other bizarre creatures. He was amazed by the sight and wanted to capture it on his canvas.

He woke up and quickly grabbed his paints and brushes. He started to paint what he remembered from his dream, but he soon realized that he had a problem. He could not paint everything that he saw, because there was too much detail and too many colors. He tried to simplify his painting, but he felt that he was losing the essence of his dream. He became frustrated and unhappy.

He decided to seek help from a wise old painter who lived nearby. He showed him his painting and told him about his dream. The old painter looked at his painting and smiled.

"My young friend, you have a gift of dreaming. You can see things that others cannot. But you also have a challenge of painting. You cannot paint everything that you see, because your canvas is limited. You have to make choices and use your creativity. You have to find a way to express your dream in your own style."

The young painter was curious and asked, "How can I do that?"

The old painter said, "There is no one answer to that question. Every painter has to find his or her own way. But I can give you some advice. Do not try to copy your dream exactly. Instead, try to capture the feeling and the meaning of your dream. Use symbols, metaphors, and associations. Mix and match different elements. Experiment with shapes, colors, and perspectives. Be playful and adventurous. Do not worry about logic or realism. Let your imagination guide you. That is the essence of surrealism."

The young painter thanked the old painter and went back to his studio. He looked at his painting again and felt a new inspiration. He started to paint over his old painting, using the old painter's advice. He painted a lion with a human face, but he also gave it a crown and a cloak, to symbolize its power and dignity. He painted a tree with eyes and mouths, but he also made it look like a musical instrument, to symbolize its harmony and expression. He painted a fish with wings, but he also added a clock and a key, to symbolize its freedom and mystery. He painted many other things, using his own symbols and metaphors. He created a new painting that was different from his dream, but also captured its feeling and meaning.

He was very happy with his new painting and showed it to the old painter. The old painter was impressed and praised him.

"You have done a wonderful job, my young friend. You have painted your dream in your own way. You have created a masterpiece of surrealism. You are a true dream painter."

The young painter was overjoyed and thanked the old painter. He continued to paint his dreams, using his creativity and imagination. He became a famous and respected painter, and his paintings inspired many people. He never forgot the old painter's advice, and he always followed his dreams.

The Happy Gardener (Epicureanism)

Once upon a time, there was a gardener who lived in a small village. He had a simple but happy life. He loved to grow fruits and vegetables in his garden, and he shared them with his friends and neighbors. He enjoyed the beauty of nature and the company of good people. He was not greedy or ambitious, but rather content and grateful.

One day, a rich merchant came to the village. He saw the gardener's garden and was impressed by its abundance and variety. He offered to buy the gardener's garden for a large sum of money. He said, "You are wasting your time and talent here. You could be rich and famous if you sell me your garden. You could travel the world and see many wonders. You could buy anything you want and have any pleasure you desire. You could live a life of luxury and happiness."

The gardener listened to the merchant's words and thought for a while. He said, "Thank you for your offer, but I must decline. I do not need your money or your pleasures. I have everything I need and want in my garden. I have the fruits and vegetables that I grow, which nourish my body and satisfy my taste. I have the flowers and trees that I tend, which delight my eyes and soothe my mind. I have the birds and bees that I watch, which fill my ears and heart with joy. I have the friends and neighbors that I share with, who support me and love me. I have the peace and freedom that I cherish, which allow me to be myself and follow my own path. I have a life of simplicity and happiness."

The merchant was surprised and puzzled by the gardener's answer. He said, "But don't you want more? Don't you want to experience new things and have more fun? Don't you want to be admired and respected by others? Don't you want to be happy?"

The gardener smiled and said, "I am happy. Happiness is not something that you can buy or chase. Happiness is something that you can find and cultivate. Happiness is not in the things that you have or the things that you do. Happiness is in the way that you live and the way that you think. Happiness is not in the quantity or the quality of your pleasures. Happiness is in the balance and the moderation of your desires. Happiness is not in the external or the future. Happiness is in the internal and the present. Happiness is not a goal or a destination. Happiness is a state and a journey."

The merchant did not understand the gardener's words. He shook his head and left. He continued to pursue his money and his pleasures, but he never found true happiness.

The gardener did not regret his decision. He continued to enjoy his garden and his life, and he was always happy.

The Wise Mouse and the Foolish Cat (Minimalism)

Once upon a time, there was a mouse who lived in a small hole in the wall. He had a simple but happy life. He ate the crumbs that he found on the floor, and he drank the water that he collected from the sink. He had a few things that he needed, such as a bed made of cotton, a book of stories, and a flute that he played. He was not bothered by anything or anyone.

One day, a cat moved into the house. He had a lavish but miserable life. He ate the finest food that he could find, and he drank the freshest milk that he could get. He had many things that he wanted, such as a velvet pillow, a golden collar, and a diamond ring. He was always troubled by something or someone.

The cat saw the mouse and decided to catch him. He thought, "That mouse looks so small and weak. He has nothing that I want, but he has something that I need. He has his life, and I want to take it. He will make a tasty snack for me."

The mouse saw the cat and decided to avoid him. He thought, "That cat looks so big and strong. He has everything that I don't want, but he has nothing that I need. He has his things, and I have my life. He will make a dangerous enemy for me."

The cat chased the mouse all over the house, but he could not catch him. The mouse was too fast and smart for him. The mouse ran into his hole and escaped from the cat. The cat was too slow and dumb for him. The cat scratched his paw and hurt himself.

The cat was angry and frustrated. He said, "How can this mouse be so happy? He has nothing that I have. He has no food, no drink, no pillow, no collar, no ring. He has no luxury, no comfort, no beauty. He has no happiness."

The mouse was calm and content. He said, "How can this cat be so unhappy? He has everything that I don't have. He has food, drink, pillow, collar, ring. He has luxury, comfort, beauty. He has no happiness."

The cat did not understand the mouse's words. He said, "You are a fool, mouse. You do not know what happiness is. Happiness is in having more. More things, more pleasures, more power. Happiness is in having everything."

The mouse understood the cat's words. He said, "You are a fool, cat. You do not know what happiness is. Happiness is in having enough. Enough things, enough pleasures, enough power. Happiness is in having nothing."

The cat and the mouse never agreed on what happiness was. They lived in the same house, but in different worlds. The cat continued to chase the mouse, but he never caught him. The mouse continued to avoid the cat, but he never feared him.

The cat lived a life of excess and unhappiness. The mouse lived a life of sufficiency and happiness.

The Swan and the Duckling (Dignity)

Once upon a time, there was a swan who lived in a lake. He was a beautiful and graceful bird, and he knew it. He was very proud of his appearance and his skills, and he thought that he was better than all the other birds in the lake.

One day, a duckling came to the lake. He was a small and ugly bird, and he knew it. He was very ashamed of his appearance and his skills, and he thought that he was worse than all the other birds in the lake.

The swan saw the duckling and decided to mock him. He said, "Who are you, and what are you doing here? You are the ugliest and clumsiest bird I have ever seen. You do not belong in this lake. You should go away and hide yourself."

The duckling heard the swan and felt hurt. He said, "I am sorry, I did not mean to bother you. I am just looking for a place to stay. I have no family or friends. I have nowhere else to go. Please, let me stay in this lake. I will not trouble you or anyone."

The swan was cruel and arrogant. He said, "No, you cannot stay in this lake. You are a disgrace to all the birds here. You have no beauty or grace. You have no dignity or worth. You are nothing but a nuisance and a burden."

The swan and the duckling argued and fought. The swan was rude and mean, and the duckling was polite and humble. The swan tried to chase the duckling away, and the duckling tried to find a place to hide.

But then, something unexpected happened. A hunter came to the lake, and he saw the swan and the duckling. He aimed his gun at the swan, and he said, "What a magnificent bird! He will make a fine trophy for me. I will shoot him and take him home with me."

He did not notice the duckling, and he said, "What a worthless bird! He will make no use for me. I will ignore him and leave him alone."

The swan was terrified and helpless. He said, "Help me, help me! Someone save me from the hunter! I do not want to die! I do not want to lose my beauty and grace!"

The duckling was brave and compassionate. He said, "Do not worry, do not worry! I will save you from the hunter! I do not care about your beauty and grace!"

The duckling flew out of his hiding place, and he made a loud noise. He said, "Quack, quack, quack! Look at me, look at me! I am here, I am here!"

The hunter heard the duckling, and he turned his gun away from the swan. He said, "What is that noise? Who is making that noise? Where is that noise coming from?"

The duckling flew towards the hunter, and he said, "It is me, it is me! I am making that noise! I am coming from here!"

The hunter saw the duckling, and he said, "What a foolish bird! He is flying right into my trap. I will shoot him and get rid of him."

The hunter shot the duckling, and the duckling fell to the ground. He was wounded and dying, but he was happy and proud. He said, "I did it, I did it!

I saved the swan from the hunter! I gave him a chance to live!"

The swan saw the duckling, and he felt ashamed and grateful. He said, "You did it, you did it! You saved me from the hunter! You gave me a chance to live!"

The swan flew to the duckling, and he said, "Thank you, thank you! You are a hero, you are a friend! You are the bravest and kindest bird I have ever met. You have more dignity and worth than I ever had. You are more beautiful and graceful than I ever was."

The duckling smiled and said, "You are welcome, you are welcome! You are a friend, you are a friend! You are not as bad as you seemed. You have more goodness and kindness than you showed. You are still beautiful and graceful, and you can be more."

The swan and the duckling hugged and said goodbye. The duckling died peacefully, and the swan cried sadly. The swan learned a valuable lesson. He learned that dignity is not about how you look or what you do. Dignity is about how you act and what you give. Dignity is about being respectful and helpful to others, no matter who they are or how they are. Dignity is about being true and noble to yourself, no matter what you are or how you are.

The Balloon and the Bird (Letting Go)

Once upon a time, there was a balloon who lived in a toy store. He was a bright red balloon, and he had a long string attached to him. He was very proud of his color and his string, and he thought that he was better than all the other toys in the store.

One day, a little girl came to the store and saw the balloon. She liked his color and his string, and she asked her mother to buy him. The mother agreed, and the girl took the balloon home with her. She played with him for a while, and then she tied his string to her wrist. She said, "You are my balloon, and I love you. You will always be with me, and I will never let you go."

The balloon was happy and flattered. He said, "You are my girl, and I love you too. You will always be with me, and I will never let you go."

The next day, the girl took the balloon outside with her. She wanted to show him to her friends and have fun with him. She ran and jumped and laughed, and the balloon followed her everywhere. He enjoyed the fresh air and the sunshine, and he felt free and happy.

But then, he saw something that made him curious. He saw a bird flying in the sky. The bird was blue and white, and he had wings and feathers. He looked graceful and beautiful, and he sang a sweet song. The balloon wanted to talk to him and be his friend.

He said to the girl, "Can you please untie me from your wrist? I want to fly with the bird and say hello to him."

The girl was surprised and sad. She said, "No, I can't do that. You are my balloon, and I love you. You will always be with me, and I will never let you go."

The balloon was disappointed and angry. He said, "But I want to go. You are my girl, and I love you too. But you can't keep me here forever. I want to see the world and meet new friends. I want to be free and happy."

The girl was stubborn and selfish. She said, "No, you can't go. You are mine, and you belong to me. You can't see the world and meet new friends. You can only be with me and do what I say. You can't be free and happy."

The balloon and the girl argued and fought. They both wanted their own way, and they both refused to let go. They did not realize that their string was getting weaker and weaker, and that it was about to break.

Suddenly, the string snapped, and the balloon flew away from the girl. He was free, but he was not happy. He felt scared and lonely. He did not know where he was going, or what he would find. He wished he could go back to the girl, and say sorry to her.

The girl was shocked and sad. She lost her balloon, and she could not get him back. She felt guilty and regretful. She realized that she was wrong, and that she should have let him go. She wished she could see him again, and say sorry to him.

The balloon and the girl never saw each other again. They both learned a hard lesson. They learned that love is not about holding on, but about letting go. They learned that freedom is not about doing what you want, but about doing what is right. They learned that happiness is not about having everything, but about being grateful for what you have.

The Butterfly and the Caterpillar (Shortness of Life)

Once upon a time, there was a butterfly who lived in a garden. He was a beautiful and colorful insect, and he loved to fly and explore. He had a short but happy life. He knew that he only had a few days to live, so he made the most of every moment.

One day, he met a caterpillar who lived on a leaf. He was a plain and dull insect, and he loved to eat and sleep. He had a long but boring life. He did not know that he could become a butterfly, so he wasted his time on trivial things.

The butterfly saw the caterpillar and decided to talk to him. He said, "Hello, friend. What are you doing here? You are missing out on the wonders of the garden. You should come with me and see the world. You should fly and have fun."

The caterpillar heard the butterfly and felt annoyed. He said, "Leave me alone, stranger. I am busy here. I have to eat this leaf and grow bigger. I have to prepare for the winter and survive. I have to live and have security."

The butterfly was surprised and sad. He said, "But why do you do that? You are wasting your life on meaningless things. You have no joy or adventure. You have no purpose or passion. You have no life and have nothing."

The caterpillar was angry and proud. He said, "But how can you say that? You are risking your life on foolish things. You have no safety or stability. You have no plan or future. You have no life and have nothing."

The butterfly and the caterpillar argued and fought. The butterfly was cheerful and free, and the caterpillar was gloomy and bound. The butterfly tried to persuade the caterpillar to join him, and the caterpillar tried to convince the butterfly to stay with him.

But then, something inevitable happened. A bird came to the garden, and he saw the butterfly and the caterpillar. He was hungry and greedy, and he wanted to eat them. He said, "What a tasty meal! I will have them both. I will catch them and devour them."

He noticed the butterfly, and he said, "What a beautiful insect! He will be a delicious treat for me. I will chase him and catch him."

He did not notice the caterpillar, and he said, "What a boring insect! He will be a bland snack for me. I will ignore him and leave him."

The butterfly was aware and ready. He said, "Watch out, watch out! There is a bird coming for us! He wants to eat us! We have to escape!"

The caterpillar was unaware and unprepared. He said, "What are you talking about? There is no bird coming for us. He does not care about us. We have nothing to fear."

The butterfly flew away from the leaf, and he said, "Follow me, follow me! I will show you the way to safety! I will help you to survive!"

The caterpillar stayed on the leaf, and he said, "Stay here, stay here! I will show you the way to security! I will help you to live!"

The butterfly and the caterpillar parted ways. The butterfly was fast and smart, and the caterpillar was slow and dumb. The butterfly dodged the bird, and the caterpillar faced the bird.

The bird chased the butterfly, but he could not catch him. The butterfly was too agile and clever for him. The butterfly escaped from the bird, and he was safe and happy. He said, "I did it, I did it! I avoided the bird and saved myself! I still have a chance to live!"

The bird caught the caterpillar, and he ate him. The caterpillar was too sluggish and foolish for him. The caterpillar died by the bird, and he was gone and forgotten. He said, "I failed, I failed! I could not escape the bird and save myself! I had no chance to live!"

The butterfly and the caterpillar never saw each other again. They both faced the same fate. They both learned a different lesson. They learned that life is short and uncertain. They learned that life is what you make of it. They learned that life is not about how long you live, but about how well you live. They learned that life is not about having nothing, but about doing something.

The Ant and the Grasshopper (Live at the Moment)

Once upon a time, there was an ant who lived in a colony. He was a hardworking and diligent insect, and he loved to collect and store food. He had a long and busy life. He always thought about the future and planned ahead. He never wasted his time on anything else.

One day, he met a grasshopper who lived in the field. He was a carefree and cheerful insect, and he loved to sing and dance. He had a short and easy life. He always enjoyed the present and lived in the moment. He never worried about anything else.

The ant saw the grasshopper and decided to scold him. He said, "What are you doing here? You are wasting your time on useless things. You should work hard and save food. You should prepare for the winter and survive. You should be responsible and prudent."

The grasshopper heard the ant and felt amused. He said, "Why do you do that? You are missing your time on boring things. You should relax and have fun. You should enjoy the summer and live. You should be happy and free."

The ant and the grasshopper argued and fought. The ant was serious and strict, and the grasshopper was playful and loose. The ant tried to teach the grasshopper to work, and the grasshopper tried to teach the ant to play.

But then, something inevitable happened. The winter came to the field, and it brought cold and snow. It was a harsh and cruel season, and it threatened to kill them. It said, "I am here, and I am powerful. I will take away your food and your warmth. I will end your life and your fun."

It noticed the ant, and it said, "What a smart insect! He has worked hard and saved food. He has prepared for the winter and survived. He has been responsible and prudent."

It did not notice the grasshopper, and it said, "What a foolish insect! He has relaxed and had fun. He has enjoyed the summer and lived. He has been happy and free."

The ant was ready and safe. He said, "I knew it, I knew it! The winter is here and it is dangerous. It wants to take away my food and my warmth. It wants to end my life and my fun. But I have worked hard and saved food. I have prepared for the winter and survived. I have been responsible and prudent."

The grasshopper was unready and doomed. He said, "I did not know it, I did not know it! The winter is here and it is terrible. It has taken away my food and my warmth. It has ended my life and my fun. But I have relaxed and had fun. I have enjoyed the summer and lived. I have been happy and free."

The ant and the grasshopper faced the same fate. They both died in the winter. They both learned a different lesson. They learned that life is short and uncertain. They learned that life is a balance of work and play.

They learned that life is not about preparing for the future, or enjoying the present. Life is about doing both, and finding the right measure. Life is about being responsible and prudent, and being happy and free.

A Heartfelt Thank You And A Special Request From The Author Of '110 Fables For Today's Young Readers'

Dear Readers,

I am deeply grateful for your interest and support for my book '110 Fables for Today's Young Readers'. It is a collection of stories that explore the various aspects of human nature, such as greed, love, fear, courage, and wisdomand others topics. I hope you enjoyed reading them and learned something valuable from them.

If you liked my book, I have a special request for you. Please check out my other book series 'Homo Sapiens', which is a historical and philosophical journey through the evolution of our species. It covers topics such as the origin of life, the development of culture, the rise and fall of civilizations, the impact of technology, and the future of humanity and other topics. It is a fascinating and enlightening read that will challenge your assumptions and broaden your perspective.

You can find all the books in the 'Homo Sapiens' series on Amazon, Flipkart, or any other online bookstore. I would appreciate it if you could leave a review or rating for them, as it would help me reach more readers and share my vision. Thank you so much for your time and attention.

Sincerely,

Mawphniang Napoleon

About The Author

P.C : Clarissa C Giri K

Mawphniang Napoleon is a man of many talents and passions. A lawyer and entrepreneur by profession, he is also a writer and humanist by passion. He is a soul ever-striving, never at ease, with boundless curiosity and verve. He embraces new ideas with an open mind, and ventures boldly into unknown lands. He is passionate about seeking all that life has to offer and makes the most of time's fleeting sands. His inquisitive nature knows no bounds as he seeks answers to life's enigmas. He cherishes the small things in life and is on a journey of self-discovery. He writes his story, never fearing and making the most of every moment, ever-unfurled. He is from Syadheh village, Ri Bhoi District in Meghalaya, India.

Khublei Shi Hajar Nguh

"

. . .

. . .

. . .

. . .

KHUBLEI SHI HAJAR NGUH

. . .

. . .

. . .

. . .

"